Accession no.
36159854

D1380870

MOTOR CONTROL IN EVERYDAY ACTIONS

TIMOTHY D. LEE, PHD

MCMASTER UNIVERSITY, HAMILTON, ONTARIO

LIS - LIBRARY

Date	Fund
20|04|12	s-che

Order No.

228747x

University of Chester

Human Kinetics

Library of Congress Cataloging-in-Publication Data

Lee, Timothy Donald, 1955-
  Motor control in everyday actions / Timothy D. Lee.
      p. ; cm.
  Includes bibliographical references and index.
  ISBN-13: 978-0-7360-8393-5 (hard cover)
  ISBN-10: 0-7360-8393-6 (hard cover)
  1. Movement, Psychology of. 2. Motor learning. I. Title.
  [DNLM: 1. Motor Skills. 2. Psychomotor Performance. WE 103]
  BF295.L44 2011
  152.3--dc22

2011004905

ISBN-10: 0-7360-8393-6 (print)
ISBN-13: 978-0-7360-8393-5 (print)

Copyright © 2011 by Timothy D. Lee

All rights reserved. Except for use in a review, the reproduction or utilization of this work in any form or by any electronic, mechanical, or other means, now known or hereafter invented, including xerography, photocopying, and recording, and in any information storage and retrieval system, is forbidden without the written permission of the publisher.

The web addresses cited in this text were current as of January 2011, unless otherwise noted.

Acquisitions Editor: Myles Schrag; **Developmental Editor:** Katherine Maurer; **Assistant Editor:** Steven Calderwood; **Copyeditor:** Patsy Fortney; **Permission Manager:** Dalene Reeder; **Graphic Designer:** Fred Starbird; **Graphic Artist:** Denise Lowry; **Cover Designer:** Keith Blomberg; **Photographer (cover):** Bradley Kanaris/Getty Images; **Photo Asset Manager:** Laura Fitch; **Visual Production Assistant:** Joyce Brumfield; **Photo Production Manager:** Jason Allen; **Art Manager:** Kelly Hendren; **Associate Art Manager:** Alan L. Wilborn; **Illustrations:** © Human Kinetics; **Printer:** Sheridan Books

Printed in the United States of America   10 9 8 7 6 5 4 3 2 1

The paper in this book is certified under a sustainable forestry program.

Human Kinetics
Website: www.HumanKinetics.com

United States: Human Kinetics, P.O. Box 5076, Champaign, IL 61825-5076
800-747-4457
e-mail: humank@hkusa.com

Canada: Human Kinetics, 475 Devonshire Road Unit 100, Windsor, ON N8Y 2L5
800-465-7301 (in Canada only)
e-mail: info@hkcanada.com

Europe: Human Kinetics, 107 Bradford Road, Stanningley, Leeds LS28 6AT, United Kingdom
+44 (0) 113 255 5665
e-mail: hk@hkeurope.com

Australia: Human Kinetics, 57A Price Avenue, Lower Mitcham, South Australia 5062
08 8372 0999
e-mail: info@hkaustralia.com

New Zealand: Human Kinetics, P.O. Box 80, Torrens Park, South Australia 5062
0800 222 062
e-mail: info@hknewzealand.com

E4867

For Jack L. Leavitt (1934-2007)

Friend and mentor

*"If you're not living on the edge,
you're taking up too much room."*

CONTENTS

PREFACE   IX
ACKNOWLEDGMENTS   XI

PART ONE
STORIES ABOUT PERCEPTION AND ACTION GONE WRONG 1

CHAPTER ONE   **PERCEPTUAL ERRORS** 3

THE MAGNETIC HILL   5
How do visual illusions distort perception and influence action?

THE FARMERS' MARKET   9
*What are the roles of motor error and hypervigilance in
unintended acceleration accidents?*

THE GROCERY STORE   13
*How do population stereotypes shape our interactions with
manufactured environments?*

PUSH OR PULL?   17
How do product designs influence people to perform specific actions?

CHAPTER TWO   **DECISION ERRORS** 23

FRIENDLY FIRE   25
What role did decision errors play in the death of Patrick Tillman?

METHOD TO HIS BRATNESS   27
Did John McEnroe's verbal abuse of line judges influence their decisions?

CHOKING UNDER PRESSURE   33
*What changes in information processing cause athletes
such as Jean Van de Velde to fail under pressure?*

TURN RIGHT AT THE NEXT GORILLA   39
*What is inattention blindness, and what role does it play in common
traffic accidents?*

CHAPTER THREE   **ACTION ERRORS** 43

THE CALCULATOR   45
How can product designs accommodate Fitts' law?

THE GIMME PUTT   51
Can Schmidt's law be used to predict the accuracy of golf putts?

POURING COFFEE   55
How does the information-processing rate create a speed–accuracy trade-off?

IS THE BEAN DIZZY?   59
What do Spoonerisms reveal about motor control?

PART TWO

ADVENTURES IN PERCEPTION AND ACTION..... 63

CHAPTER FOUR   **FUN WITH NUMBERS** 65

PUBLIC OPINION POLLS   67
What do central tendency, variability, and statistical significance mean in the context of motor control research?

CUTTING WOOD AND MISSING PUTTS   71
How are constant error, variable error, and absolute error useful for understanding motor control?

THE HOT HAND   75
Do statistics support the existence of hot streaks in sports?

CHAPTER FIVE   **PERCEPTION IN ACTION** 79

RED LIGHT, GREEN LIGHT   81
What factors influence reaction time and its measurement?

JUMPING THE GUN   87
How can a reaction be distinguished from an anticipation?

ANTILOCK BRAKES   91
How does the complexity of a motor program influence reaction time?

PREVENTING PENALTIES AND BATTING BASEBALLS   95
How do athletes use temporal and spatial anticipation?

CRAPS AND WEIGHTED BATS   99
What role do perceptual illusions play in sport performance?

CHAPTER SIX   **ATTENTION**. 103

THE TOAD AND THE CENTIPEDE   105
Is an internal or external attentional focus better for improving performance?

THE PRESHOT ROUTINE   109
Why does a consistent mental preparation ritual benefit performance?

GUMBO   113
What are the limits of attentional capacity?

FAKES   117
What role does the psychological refractory period play in sport?

CHAPTER SEVEN **MOTOR CONTROL** **121**

WEBSITES AND SILLY WALKS 123
How do redundancies help us solve motor problems?

THE CURLING DRAW 127
What sport skills use open- and closed-loop systems of motor control?

COOL PAPA BELL 131
When vision is interrupted, how does iconic memory guide motor tasks?

MOVING SIDEWALKS AND BEER GLASSES 135
How does the end-state comfort effect influence movement planning?

THE TICKLE 139
How do motor commands influence sensory feedback during motor control?

THE POINT OF NO RETURN 143
Is there a point in time after which an initiated motor program cannot be stopped?

FORENSIC MOTOR CONTROL 149
What are generalized motor programs, and what do keystroke dynamics reveal about them?

PARTY TRICKS 153
How does the nervous system use functional linkages to coordinate movements?

DISAPPEARING ACT 157
What makes some coordination patterns more automatic than others?

PART THREE

STORIES ABOUT LEARNING MOTOR SKILLS **161**

CHAPTER EIGHT **MEASURING MOTOR LEARNING** **163**

HOW YOU GET TO CARNEGIE HALL 165
What is the best way to measure progress in motor learning?

THE BABE 169
Can a general motor ability be defined and measured?

LEARNING TO WIN FROM LOSING 175
Why is the learning–performance distinction important?

ZERO-SUM TRAINING 179
What is the practical impact of ineffective training methods?

CHAPTER NINE **ORGANIZING PRACTICE** **181**

BUT I WAS GREAT ON THE PRACTICE RANGE! 183
How does practice repetition influence performance and learning?

THE COACH AS A DICTIONARY   187
What roles does augmented feedback play in motor learning?

THE GOLFER'S LITTLE HELPER   191
What elements of motor learning are neglected when we use mechanical training aids?

CHAPTER TEN   **SKILL DEVELOPMENT** **195**

BEND IT LIKE BECKER   197
What types of models are best to observe when learning a skill?

SPORT SNAKE OILS   201
Can visual training programs improve sport performance?

THE KEYPAD   205
How do explicit and implicit memories influence skilled performance?

WAYNE GRETZKY   209
What role does skilled perception play in sport performance?

CHAPTER ELEVEN   **SKILL RETENTION** **213**

SHOOTING TWO FROM THE LINE   215
How does the warm-up decrement affect repeated performances?

LIKE RIDING A BICYCLE   219
How are motor skills stored in memory?

H.M.   223
What does the amnesia suffered by Henry Gustav Molaison reveal about memory and motor skills?

AUTHOR INDEX   225
SUBJECT INDEX   229
ABOUT THE AUTHOR   235

PREFACE

Why did William Archibald Spooner say to a student, "You hissed my mystery lecture" and demonstrate other speech errors, now called Spoonerisms? Was John McEnroe really such a brat, or was there a preconceived intent when he berated umpire after umpire during his years as the world's best tennis player? Why did sprinter Jon Drummond lie down on the track and refuse to leave after being disqualified in the 100-meter world championship final? Wayne Gretzky was one of the greatest hockey players of all time, but some people believe that his individual skills were just average. So, what made him so great? Tiger Woods is probably the best golfer ever, but the average player would probably gain more from watching a poor golfer than from watching Tiger. And, by the way, do you feel any safer now that many states and provinces have banned the use of handheld cell phones while driving? You shouldn't.

These stories, and the others contained in this book, were written for a purpose. After 30 years of teaching and publishing research about how humans control and learn motor skills, I now realize that translating the findings of this research into our understanding of everyday life remains a challenge. One could say that we study motor control to understand how the central nervous system achieves a goal through movement, and does so in a manner that is efficient and assured. One could say that we study motor learning to understand how the brain adapts to experience in a manner that improves efficiency and assuredness. But these terms and concepts seem abstract and distant unless we understand something about the research process and the application of research findings to our everyday lives.

Few research areas are more real and day-to-day than motor control and learning. Driving to work, using a cell phone, typing these words on a new laptop—these are just some of the activities that we do almost every waking moment of our lives. They are fascinating to study, and the people who research motor control and learning are just trying to understand how we do these things. My hope is that this book will share with you some of the reasons they want to understand these things and that it will enhance your understanding of how we interact with the world.

My strategy in this book is to describe why and how researchers study motor control issues by relating (sometimes humorous) stories about the actions of people in everyday life. My intention is to present our daily experiences of moving around playing fields, freeways, and our home and work

eBook available at HumanKinetics.com

environments. Some stories are curious anecdotes, and others are about how famous people, and you and I, perform motor skills in various situations and environments. These stories illustrate the diversity and complexity of perception and action research and, hopefully, will also encourage you to think more deeply about issues such as the reasons why George Russell Weller drove his car through a crowded Santa Monica farmers' market, killing 10 people and injuring 63 others.

My undergraduate classes at McMaster University have read early drafts of this book over the past few years. One of the gratifying outcomes has been that these stories have generated a lot of interest—not only in the topics of the stories but also in the underlying fundamental concepts involving perception, action, and learning. Some of these students have even used the stories as springboards for the development of their own research studies. It pleases me that these stories provided a little perspective that went a very long way in overcoming some of the barriers to thinking about research.

In the end, you may not resonate with all of the stories in this book. However, if some or even just one of them motivates you to want to learn more about the research associated with the story, then I consider my goal achieved. The Notes and Suggested Readings sections at the end of each story will help you to find out more about the research. I hope this is just the beginning of your research quest.

Acknowledgments

This book has been in progress for a long time. Starting out as a list of ideas about perception and action, each story has undergone many changes along the way, and I owe a debt of gratitude to the people who helped to shape the final product. Draft copies of it were used for my kinesiology course Adventures in Perception and Action over the past few years, and the students were wonderful in providing many suggestions. Andrea Swanson suggested a layout that maintains a consistent framework among the chapters and helped to structure my writing. Dick Schmidt and Ron Marteniuk, two giants in the field of motor control and learning, read early drafts of the book and made many excellent suggestions for improvement. Judy Wright at Human Kinetics was a huge supporter of the project from the very beginning and offered many tips on improving the content. Kate Maurer, developmental editor at Human Kinetics, was superb in shaping the manuscript into the form that you see now. And Laurie Wishart, my frequent research collaborator, best friend, and wife, provided continued motivation for the project from day one. I would not, nor could not, have done it without her support.

PART ONE

STORIES ABOUT PERCEPTION AND ACTION GONE WRONG

Each case is oddly familiar. Everything is normal at the start—the driver gets into the car, puts the key into the ignition, starts the engine, applies the right foot to the brake pedal, and then moves the automatic gear shift lever from Park into Drive or Reverse. What happens next is a chaotic nightmare. The car lurches from its stationary position, sometimes leaving a patch of rubber on the pavement, and rapidly accelerates to faster and faster speeds. The driver realizes that something has gone wrong, and panic quickly sets in as the driver wonders, *Why is the car moving? My foot is on the brake!* The only conclusion that comes to mind is that the brakes have failed, so the panicked driver responds by pumping the brake pedal or just pushing it harder and harder. In many cases the pedal is pushed all the way to the floor. But the car does not slow down. Just the opposite—it goes faster. The driver is now in such a panicked state that the most logical way to stop the car—by turning off the ignition—never enters the driver's mind. Instead, the driver continues to push on the completely ineffective pedal. In the end, something else stops the car, such as a tree, a building, or another vehicle. If the driver is lucky, the damage is minimal. But, all too often, the car does not stop until someone is badly hurt, or in one case, after 10 people have died and many dozens more have been left injured (see "The Farmers' Market" in chapter 1).

Many, if not most, of these tragic accidents are believed to have resulted from a similar cause—human error. In these types of accidents, the driver's foot is mistakenly placed on the gas pedal rather than the brake pedal. Therefore, the car immediately accelerates when the automatic transmission is engaged in Drive (or Reverse). Unaware of the error in foot placement, the driver pushes harder and harder on what is believed to be the brake but is actually the gas pedal. And so begins a tragic sequence of events in which the driver's attempt to stop the car actually worsens the situation.

These episodes of what is called unintended acceleration are believed to arise from fundamental errors involving human perception and action, which are then compounded further by the panic that overcomes the driver. But, in typical cases of unintended acceleration and in other situations we will consider, many things were done correctly. The foot responded correctly to the brain's command to press harder on the pedal. The car responded correctly to what the foot instructed it to do. And yet, the result was not as the driver had intended. How could this happen?

In part I, Stories about Perception and Action Gone Wrong, I discuss some of the errors that occur as we move about in our world. Although it is not always possible to know with complete confidence why or how an error occurred, often there is ample evidence to suspect a cause or an underlying rationale that led to the error. Some of these errors are nothing more than aggravations, such as light switches that do not respond as we expect them to, or ceiling fans that tell us little about which string operates which function. Other errors have more tragic consequences—such as incidents of friendly fire and unintended acceleration.

I have divided the stories in this part into chapters that address problems in perception, decision making, and action. However, be aware that human errors often evolve into a sequence of events that involve all of these cognitive activities.

CHAPTER ONE

PERCEPTUAL ERRORS

We move about in a complex and sometimes cluttered environment. Most of the time our minds provide us with a faithful representation of that environment, but not always. The story "The Magnetic Hill" discusses illusions, some natural and some contrived, that reveal discrepancies between what we perceive and how we act on those perceptions. Although some of these illusions and misperceptions are fun and funny, cases of unintended acceleration are not. The story "The Farmers' Market" describes one such tragedy and a trial that presented two very different accounts about how and why the accident occurred. Manufacturers take great pleasure in designing products that are aesthetically pleasing. However, the design flaws presented in "The Grocery Store" and "Push or Pull?" remind us that even simple products are sometimes designed without considering the best interests of the people who must actually use them.

THE MAGNETIC HILL

How do visual illusions distort perception and influence action?

There is a place in New Brunswick, Canada, to which people travel to be fooled. They call it a magnetic hill. People drive to a certain location on a country road, put their car in neutral, and watch in amazement as it begins to roll *up* the hill. Or, at least, that is what seems to happen. The hill is not magnetic, of course, and the car does not actually go uphill. But the feeling of rolling uphill is there just the same.

We depend on vision to interpret the world around us, using perceptual skills learned over a lifetime of experiences and interactions with our environment. But, our visual perception can sometimes be fooled, and researchers find this very exciting because it leads to fascinating insights regarding how we think and act. The magnetic hill is one of many types of visual illusions—examples of how perception can lead us to mistaken conclusions about reality. An important lesson about the magnetic hill illusion is that what we see often overshadows what we feel.

There are scores of visual illusions, and scientists have been studying them for many years. One of the better known and most often studied of these is called the Müller-Lyer illusion, which is illustrated in figure 1.1. Compare the two lines in the figure. The line between the tails (i.e., > and <) in the figure on the left looks longer than the line in the figure on the right. In reality, the lines are identical in length; the orientation of the inward- and outward-pointing tails, in relation to the line, creates the illusion that the lines are unequal. Your perception of reality has been fooled, not unlike what happens at the magnetic hill.

Visual illusions can lead us not only to see things that are not real, but also to feel things that are not real, such as what occurs in the size–weight illusion. You can readily experience this illusion by filling two containers, one smaller than the other, with equal amounts of mass (e.g., sand). Then, ask a

Figure 1.1 Two figures showing the Müller-Lyer illusion. The horizontal line on the left appears longer to most people than the line on the right. However, they are the same length.

friend to lift both containers, one at a time, and tell you which one is heavier. After lifting each of the containers, most people perceive that the smaller container is heavier than the larger container. Of course, you know this is wrong because you filled them with equal amounts of sand.

The key to experiencing the illusion depends on seeing the difference in the size of the containers. After many years of experiencing objects of different sizes, we have come to the general conclusion that bigger objects are heavier than smaller objects. The visual difference between the sizes of the two containers has set up, or biased, our motor system to expect something that we have previously experienced to be true. When we pick up the two containers (which are identical in mass), the expectation is that the larger one *should be* heavier than the smaller one. When this fails to be confirmed (because they actually weigh the same), most people conclude that something unexpected is occurring and therefore they perceive, incorrectly, that the smaller object must weigh more than the larger object.

The size–weight illusion is strongest when we allow our visual system to bias our expectations. However, the work of neuroscientist Randy Flanagan and others suggests that the size–weight illusion remains strong even after subjects are told, quite explicitly, that the smaller and larger objects weigh exactly the same. And more surprising, their research revealed that the perceptual illusion remained as strong after 20 lifts of the two equally weighted objects: repeatedly lifting the two objects fails to bring perception any closer to the truth. However, there is one special finding to note about their research: the hands quickly adjusted to the illusion by changing their grip. Initially, the subjects were using a stronger grip force with the smaller

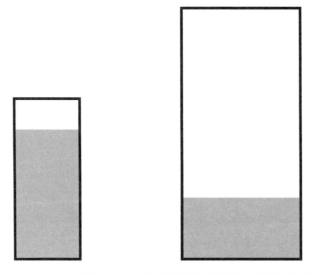

Figure 1.2   The size–weight illusion. Which of these two containers is heavier? When filled with equal amounts of mass (e.g., sand) so that they weigh exactly the same, the smaller container will feel heavier than the larger container.

object than they used with the larger object, consistent with what the visual system "told" the hand to do. However, after just a few trials, the subjects were using equivalent grip forces to lift the two containers. In other words, the motor system adjusted quickly to the reality that the objects were equal in weight even though the subjects' perception continued to be fooled by the visual illusion.

The size–weight illusion tells us something very interesting about the interaction of our visual, motor, and cognitive systems. One suggestion is that we tend to believe our eyes more than our limbs. But perhaps what is more interesting about visual illusions is that our conscious perception of reality can be tricked more easily than our actions.

These illusions reveal that vision dominates what we see and feel, distorting our sense of reality. So, what about our other senses, such as hearing—does vision bias what we hear as well? Researchers who study the McGurk effect suggest so. Initially investigated by Harry McGurk and his colleague John MacDonald, subjects in their study viewed close-up films of a woman's head as she uttered a single-syllable word. The movements of her lips clearly showed her saying the syllable "ga," but the vocal track that the subject heard was the syllable "ba." Indeed, people who watched the film without the soundtrack reported that they saw "ga," and people who listened to the auditory track without watching the video reported that they heard "ba." So, did the subjects report "ga" or "ba" when the soundtrack and video were played simultaneously? As it turns out, most people reported hearing neither of those two syllables. Instead, they reported that the woman had said "da"—an incorrect hybrid perception of what was seen and heard.

The McGurk effect is a nice illustration of the fact that our perception of reality actually results from a combination of inputs from our senses. When one of those senses gets fooled, especially when it involves vision, our combined perception is likely to be fooled as well. And the strength of these illusions indicates that our visual system will continue to fool us for a period of time after we experience reality. The magnetic hill just happens to be one of those perceptual illusions that nature provides to keep us on our toes.

SELF-DIRECTED LEARNING ACTIVITIES

1. Define *illusion* in your own words.

2. Describe a real-life experience in which you encountered a visual illusion. What was the reality, and what were you fooled into believing?

3. Find a research article in the literature in which the effect of an illusion on visual perception is contrasted with the effect on movement accuracy. Were the effects on perception and action similar or different?

4. Design a research experiment that explores the role of actions in a different type of visual illusion (e.g., the Titchener illusion or the Ponzo illusion—for some examples, see Schmidt & Lee, 2011, figure 5.2).

NOTES

- There are a number of online videos demonstrating the McGurk effect. This one is a particularly good illustration:

  www.tinyurl.com/mcgurkeffectyoutube

SUGGESTED READINGS

Flanagan, J.R., & Beltzner, M.A. (2000). Independence of perceptual and sensorimotor predictions in the size–weight illusion. *Nature Neuroscience, 3,* 737-741.

McGurk, H., & MacDonald, J. (1976). Hearing lips and seeing voices. *Nature, 264,* 747-748.

Rosenblum, L.D. (2005). The primacy of multimodal speech perception. In D. Pisoni & R. Remez (Eds.), *Handbook of speech perception* (pp. 51–78). Malden, MA: Blackwell.

Rosenblum, L.D. (2008). Speech perception as a multimodal phenomenon. *Current Directions in Psychological Science, 17,* 405-409.

Schmidt, R.A., & Lee, T.D. (2011). Sensory contributions to motor control. In *Motor control and learning: A behavioral emphasis* (5th ed., pp. 135-176). Champaign, IL: Human Kinetics.

What are the roles of motor error and hypervigilance in unintended acceleration accidents?

Santa Monica is located in west Los Angeles, along the strip of land that borders the Pacific Ocean. It is home to movie stars, sports heroes, and many wonderful entertainment and shopping venues. One day each week a multiblock section of Santa Monica is barricaded from traffic and hosts an open-air farmers' market, where vendors from near and far come to sell food, clothing, jewelry, and other goods to the many thousands who gather in the area. On July 16, 2003, 86-year-old George Russell Weller drove his Buick LeSabre through the crowds of people who were shopping at the farmers' market, killing 10 and injuring 63. This story concerns why it happened.

The prosecution, at Weller's trial several years later, claimed it was no accident—that Weller deliberately drove his car through the crowded market. The reason, they said, was that Weller had been involved in a minor fender bender just moments before he entered the farmers' market. His response to the fender bender was to flee the scene of the accident. Witnesses for the prosecution painted Weller as a cold-blooded killer, commenting on the determined look on his face during the ordeal and his relatively calm demeanor afterward. It probably also didn't help his case when he emerged from the car immediately afterward and wondered aloud why the people he had hit had not jumped out of his way. Adding his age into the mix, Weller's actions were painted as rather pathetic.

Richard Schmidt, a renowned motor control scholar and human factors expert, testified on behalf of the defense team and argued that the facts of the case shared many similarities to accidents caused by errors of pedal misapplication, or unintended acceleration. Accidents of this type, which, thankfully, are quite rare, occur when the driver intends to apply pressure to the brake pedal, but misses the brake and pushes down on the accelerator instead.

Unintended acceleration accidents had been investigated for many years prior to the Weller case. These accidents were more common when the driver first got into the car, started the engine, and engaged the automatic transmission from the Park position into either Drive or Reverse. Indeed, such frequent episodes of "runaway cars" were the primary reason auto manufacturers added the brake–transmission shift interlock system in the 1980s so that an automatic transmission lever could not be moved from the Park position until the car sensed that a certain amount of pressure had been applied to the brake. However, the brake lock system only prevented this particular type of pedal misapplication; moving the foot to the accelerator instead of the brake would not be prevented once the transmission was successfully engaged out of Park and the car was in motion.

It is important to note that reaching for the brake requires that we steer the foot from a comfortable seated position to a target (the brake) in the absence of any visual guidance. We do this all the time without making any errors. We know where the brake is located from experience, and we also know that the brake feels different underfoot than does the accelerator. So then why would we suddenly miss the brake, push down on the accelerator instead, and then keep the foot there?

Schmidt (1989) presented evidence that unintended acceleration cases frequently involved accidents in which the driver had less experience than usual with that particular vehicle. Therefore, in some of these cases, the exact location and feel of the brake might not have been as familiar to the driver as normally could have been expected. These accidents also occurred more frequently on start-up, compared to later in the driving cycle, perhaps due to temporary factors associated with preparing an action (see "Shooting Two From the Line" in chapter 11). Driver inattention has also been linked with these cases, so it may not come as a surprise that drivers would not immediately notice the difference between the brake and gas pedal if engaged in a distracting activity at the same time (see "Gumbo" in chapter 6).

But for Weller, none of the common profiles for these accidents fit the case: he had already been driving before the supposed pedal misapplication error, so it was not a matter of missing the brake on initial start-up. Weller was quite familiar with his own vehicle, an 11-year-old Buick LeSabre. And he was not talking on a cell phone. Instead, Schmidt argued that Weller's pedal misapplication error was likely triggered by a catastrophic case of panic, termed hypervigilance, which could have been initiated when Weller had been involved in the fender bender just prior to the episode.

But one last issue seemed particularly problematic, according to the prosecution. Once the pedal misapplication error had occurred and the car started to accelerate wildly out of control, why didn't Weller simply remove his foot from the pedal or turn off the engine—actions that would have brought the car quickly to a stop? Again, failure to carry out corrective actions is typical of unintended acceleration cases, and some reasonable accounts have been offered to explain why drivers do not perform them. First, the driver probably does not realize that the foot is on the accelerator rather than the brake. The intention was to press the brake, and the fact that the pedal has gone all the way to the floor could reasonably be interpreted as brake failure rather than human error. And second, once the driver enters into this catastrophic state of panic, all normal modes of thinking cease. Reasoning and problem solving, the kinds of activities that are easy to do when unflustered, become unlikely, if not impossible, to carry out when in this state of hypervigilance.

Thomas Shelton, a member of the California Highway Patrol, testified at Weller's trial that he once investigated an unintended acceleration case in which an elderly woman ended up driving her car onto the top of another vehicle. The woman was in such a panicked state that when Shelton arrived at the accident scene, he had to climb up into the car to shut off the racing engine, at which time he noticed that the woman was still seated, very much alive, staring straight ahead with a death grip on the steering wheel, and with her foot still pushing the accelerator all the way to the floor.

Unfortunately, all of these arguments can only be used to speculate about what may have occurred in George Russell Weller's Buick LeSabre on that fateful day. On October 20, 2006, the jury convicted him of vehicular manslaughter in the 10 deaths resulting from the Santa Monica farmers' market crash. Nobody will ever know whether the verdict was the right one.

SELF-DIRECTED LEARNING ACTIVITIES

1. In your own words describe the phenomenon known as unintended acceleration.

2. Describe a situation in which you made an action error that you were able to correct. How did you know that you had made the error, and what did you do to correct it?

3. Using our feet to manipulate car pedals involves aiming without visual feedback. What factors influence our ability to make these aiming movements accurately?

4. Propose a research methodology that examines one's ability to (a) move to a target without visual feedback and (b) estimate the accuracy of those aimed movements (again, without vision).

NOTES

- Evidence from George Weller's trial during September and October of 2006 was summarized in the *Santa Monica Daily Press*, which can be accessed through its archives:

    www.tinyurl.com/wellertrial

- Not all cases of unintended acceleration are generally agreed to be the result of a pedal misapplication. A segment of the television show *60 Minutes*, hosted by Ed Bradley and which aired November 22, 1986, claimed that accidents of similar etiology involving the Audi 5000 were the result of a faulty idle stabilizer, which caused the car to accelerate wildly out of control when put into gear. An investigation by the U.S. NHTSA (National Highway Traffic Safety Administration) failed to support *60 Minutes'* claim.

- More recently, runaway Toyotas have been a topic of concern. Once again, a government investigation failed to support a claim that these cases of unintended acceleration were due to an electronic fault in the engine. Again, this leaves open the very real possibility that driver error is to blame, as suggested by Richard Schmidt in the New York Times:

  www.tinyurl.com/schmidtnyt

SUGGESTED READINGS

Castelli, J., Nash, C., Ditlow, C., & Pecht, M. (2003). *Sudden acceleration: The myth of driver error.* University of Maryland: CALCE EPSC Press.

Pollard, J., & Sussman, E.D. (1989). *An examination of sudden acceleration.* National Highway Traffic Safety Administration Final Report # DOT-TSC-NHTSA-89-1.

Schmidt, R.A. (1989). Unintended acceleration: A review of human factors contributions. *Human Factors, 31,* 345-364.

Schmidt, R.A. (1993). Unintended acceleration: Human performance considerations. In B. Peacock & W. Karwowski (Eds.), *Automotive ergonomics* (pp. 431-451). London: Taylor & Francis.

Schmidt, R.A., & Lee, T.D. (2011). Central contributions to motor control. In *Motor control and learning: A behavioral emphasis* (5th ed., pp. 177-222) Champaign, IL: Human Kinetics.

How do population stereotypes shape our interactions with manufactured environments?

A new grocery store opened near my home a little while ago, and for periods of time I watched with bemusement as shoppers tried to enter the store. Many went to the automatic door, which would not open automatically, looked up, backed up, and then went over to the other set of doors to enter. What was the problem? In this case, the problem was simple: as you approached the store from the parking lot, the doors to enter the store were on the *left*, and the doors to exit were on the *right*. North Americans have spent a lifetime learning to do just the opposite. Highways and bicycle lanes are set up so that you pass to the right of oncoming traffic. Uncrowded sidewalks and hallways are the same. And when someone violates that principle, it results in an awkward little dance to avoid running into the other person. Most stores are set up similarly—as you approach the store the set of doors to enter are located on the right and the doors on the left are used for people exiting the store. The store that opened near me violated a simple principle, called a *population stereotype*—a type of habit.

Think about some of the other strong population stereotypes in North American culture. People tend to flip a switch up to turn lights on, and down to turn lights off. The color red usually means "stop," or refers to danger, whereas green means "go" or "safe." Turning a dial clockwise usually means

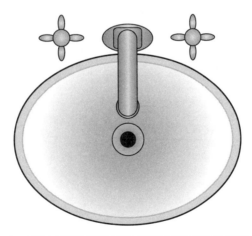

Figure 1.3 Typical hot and cold water taps in a bathroom sink. Which way would you turn them to start the flow of water—both to the left, both to the right, both inward, or both outward?

to increase the value of something; turning it counterclockwise decreases it. Notice that these examples refer to manufactured products. However, other features of our manufactured environment are less stereotypical. For example, look at the faucets in figure 1.3. There is a strong stereotype in North American society to associate the left faucet with hot water and the right faucet with cold water. But, which way would you turn the left and right knobs to start the flow of water? Both clockwise? Both counterclockwise? Or would you turn them in opposite directions, and if so, how (both inward or both outward)? The stereotype for controlling the flow of water is not nearly as strong as the stereotype for hot on the left and cold on the right.

We had the master bathroom in our house remodeled a short time ago and gave the designer some artistic freedom with some of the details. Figure 1.4 is a drawing of how the bathtub faucets are now arranged (viewed from above). The faucets are illustrated in the upper left corner. Which ones do you think control the hot and cold water? To this day I still have no idea which controls which, not to mention which way to turn the knobs to get the water flowing.

Strong population stereotypes have both positive and negative consequences. For example, knowing that hot water will flow from the tap

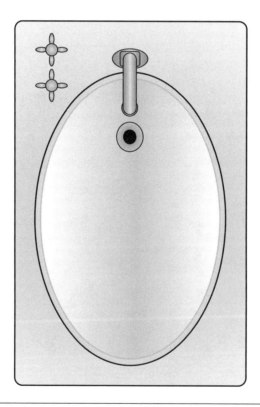

Figure 1.4   Our redesigned bathroom tub. Which tap controls the hot water, and which way should the knobs be turned to start and stop the flow of water?

on the left makes the operation of the taps simpler and more efficient, and reduces the need for signs and labels to tell you how to use them. However, the occurrence of strong population stereotypes can also lead to errors or accidents when someone violates them. And they can lead to *many* mistakes when an interface is designed so that a correct action is in violation of the stereotype. Arranging doors in a public place in violation of a strong population stereotype, as the grocery store near me did, is an open invitation to accidents.

SELF-DIRECTED LEARNING ACTIVITIES

1. Define the term *population stereotype* in your own words.
2. Identify three strong population stereotypes that are different in North America than in another part of the world. Suggest a reason or hypothesis for why they are different.
3. Design a questionnaire with questions about daily actions for which you think population stereotypes might exist; then have 20 or more people respond to it. What items in the questionnaire revealed strong stereotypes, and what items revealed weak stereotypes?
4. Design a research study that investigates the comparative strength of two population stereotypes. Be careful to explain what behavior is measured in your experiment, and why this measure allows you to make conclusions about stereotype strength.

SUGGESTED READINGS

Barber, P.J. (1988). *Applied cognitive psychology: An information processing framework*. London: Methuen.

Jordan, P. (1998). *An introduction to usability*. London: CRC Press.

Proctor, R.W., & Van Zandt, T. (2008). *Human factors in simple and complex systems* (2nd ed.). Boca Raton, FL: CRC Press.

How do product designs influence people to perform specific actions?

It seems hard to believe, but brand-new buildings are still being constructed with very silly design features. For example, a new building on our campus opened last year and featured many modern technologies, including very nice-looking glass doors through which you enter and exit the building. The problem is that the doors have identical handles on either side. The handles themselves are very attractive, but they don't tell me what to do when I want to enter the building—should I push or pull the door? The handles on these particular doors suggest to me that they are made for grasping and pulling. However, the door goes in only one direction, and the very same handles appear on *both* sides of the door. Therefore, to enter the building, I have to use the handle to pull the door, and to exit, I have to use the identical type of handle to push the door. How would someone possibly know which way the door swings when approaching it? After a year of using these doors on a daily basis, I still just guess about whether to push or pull. Why would someone design a door like that?

Michael Darnell has created a wonderful website that illustrates many instances of products that have been designed without the user in mind. One of his web pages describes a door handle problem similar to the one I just described, in which a building has a short walkway with one set of doors on either end. Each door has identical handles on either side of the door (the same type of handle is used for pushing and pulling the door). However, according to Darnell, these particular doors were installed such that the problem was magnified even more—the doors at either end of the walkway both swung out from the walkway. He tells the story of a friend who entered the walkway by pulling on the handle of one door; then went to the second door and found that the door would not open when she pulled on the handle. So, concluding that the door was locked, she returned to the first door to exit and found herself trapped in the walkway when the door wouldn't move when she pulled on its handle. After trying to get the attention of others on the outside to tell them that she was trapped in the walkway, she finally realized, with much embarrassment, that the handles had to be pushed when inside the walkway. Darnell reminds us that this funny story could have had tragic consequences if, for example, a panicked person were trying to flee the building in case of a fire.

There are many ways to solve this problem of having identical handles used for opposite actions. One solution would be to put signs on the door that say "push" or "pull." Although these signs would probably work, a well-designed door (i.e., designed for the user rather than for its looks) should not need a sign to tell people how to use it. Pushing and pulling a door are not rocket science, after all. A better solution would be to install a flat plate on one side of the door, which would make the correct choice obvious: Because there is no handle to grab to pull toward you, there is only one other option—push! A sign would be unnecessary in this case because there would be no question about which action to take.

Signs and symbols that tell us how to use things should be the last option in technology design. Signs are sometimes small and hard to read, they fall off, they wear out, other things cover them up, and they are often presented in only one language, making them less than desirable in a multicultural society. Symbols avoid being unilingual but introduce other problems, such as ambiguity. For example, how would one create simple, unambiguous, and instantly recognizable symbols for "push" and "pull"? As in the door handle example, a better design would be one that made the correct action as obvious as possible, one that would negate the need for a sign or symbol.

A classic example of the failure of technology to exploit this simple idea is a standard topic in ergonomics textbooks and on websites: the arrangement of burners on the stove top. A typical stove top layout is shown in figure 1.5. The four knobs used to turn on the elements are located at the top of the figure. Quick, say out loud which one is used to turn on the right front burner. My guess is that it is one of the two rightmost knobs. But which one? It is impossible to know for certain without turning one of the knobs and waiting to see which element begins to heat up. So, designers add little labels to tell us which knobs are mapped to which burners. Do they work?

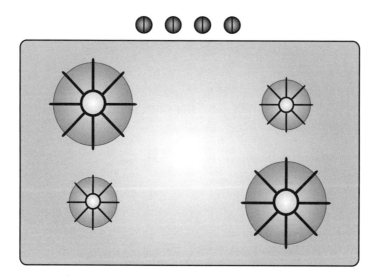

Figure 1.5　Common stove top layout. Quick, which knob controls the back left burner?

My personal experience is that these labels, if they have not fallen off, worn out, been covered by last night's pasta sauce, or been printed too small to read, are still hard to interpret. More times than I wish to remember, I have returned to a stove expecting to find a pot of boiling water for my pasta but instead found a glowing burner with nothing on it. The relative failure rate of these labels leads me to believe that they are only slightly more helpful than if I had just turned a knob at random.

Have a look at the two alternative stove top designs in figure 1.6. The layout of the knobs in figure 1.6*a* is the same as before; only the burner layout has been altered. In figure 1.6*b*, the burner layout is the same as it was before, but now the arrangement of the knobs has been altered. In

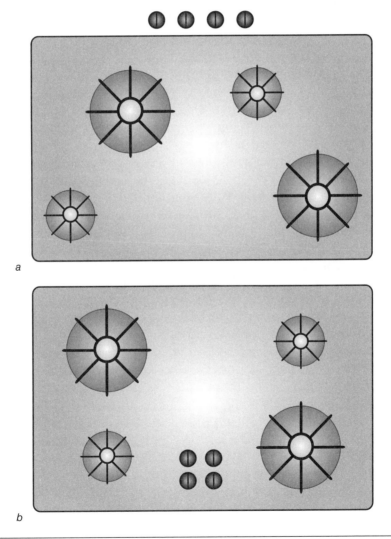

a

b

Figure 1.6 Two alternative stove top layouts. Compare these layouts to the layout in figure 1.5. Now there is no ambiguity as to which knobs control which burners.

both cases, the mapping of each knob to its associated burner has been made obvious by a simple rearrangement of either the knobs or the burner layout. No symbols or labels are needed, and the chances of turning on the wrong burner are minimal. Moreover, the amount of space occupied by the burners and knobs in these more compatible layouts is identical to the space occupied in the incompatible layout. It is interesting to note that these alternative layouts have been available for many years. But have a look at any appliance store flyer or website, and you will see that the classic design still continues to dominate the market.

Sometimes it is simply not possible to avoid the use of labels or signs. In such cases the designer's goal should be to make them as informative as possible. The typical ceiling fan is another good example of a failure to consider the needs of the user when designing the product. The ceiling fan that we have in our home has a wall switch that turns the fan off and on. But the ceiling fan has three additional controls, located on the base of the fan itself (where the fan connects to the ceiling), that are operated by pulling on long strings that hang down from the base. These three strings can be pulled to adjust the speed of the fan, to reverse its direction, or to turn off or on a light located on the bottom of the fan. The problem is that the strings are identical in appearance; I have no way of knowing which control I am activating when I pull on any of the strings.

Actually, that is not completely true. If I stand on a stepladder and get up really close to the ceiling, I can see little labels beside the holes where the strings exit the electrical base of the fan that say "speed," "light," and "direction." I could also stand on the floor and use binoculars to read these labels, I suppose. But, you get the point. Because these labels are next to useless to me, I really just have a one-in-three chance of getting it right each time I pull one of the strings.

How could each control be designed to communicate its function easily to the user? I have used two strategies to modify my own fan. Because reversing the fan's direction is the control that I use least often, I have shortened the string associated with this option to be the most difficult of the three to reach. However, I use the light and speed options about equally often. So, to make these as distinct as possible I borrowed two charms from an old charm bracelet and attached them to the ends of each string. A charm of a rabbit is attached to the string that controls the speed of the fan, and a charm of a book (for which I turn on the light to read) is attached to the string that controls the light. The fan may not look the way the manufacturer had intended it to look, but I have not made the mistake of pulling the wrong string since I attached these charms.

Motor skills such as pushing doors, turning knobs, and pulling strings are simple to learn, and we have all mastered these simple skills over our lifetimes. So why do we have such trouble using them? One reason is that the manufacturer is often paying more attention to aesthetics than to the needs of the user.

SELF-DIRECTED LEARNING ACTIVITIES

1. Describe, in general, the principle of how product design influences human performance.

2. Search the literature for the term *stimulus–response compatibility*; then define it in your own words with specific reference to an example presented in this story.

3. Over the next 24 hours, keep a diary of all the objects or things you encounter that you think represent stimulus–response *in*compatibility. Propose ways each of these things could be made more compatible.

4. Find three research articles in which stimulus–response compatibility has been investigated. What are the similarities and differences in the stimuli and responses used in these studies?

NOTES

- Michael Darnell has a wonderful website that features many examples of poorly designed products, with suggestions about simple ways to greatly improve usability:
  www.baddesigns.com

SUGGESTED READINGS

Proctor, R.W., & Van Zandt, T. (2008). *Human factors in simple and complex systems* (2nd ed.). Boca Raton, FL: CRC Press.

Proctor, R.W., & Vu, K.P.L. (2006). *Stimulus-response compatibility principles: Data, theory, and application*. Boca Raton, FL: CRC Press.

Schmidt, R.A., & Lee, T.D. (2011). Human information processing. In *Motor control and learning: A behavioral emphasis* (5th ed., pp. 57-96) Champaign, IL: Human Kinetics.

DECISION ERRORS

Many of life's little frustrations occur when we do things exactly as we intended to do them, but the result is not what we wanted. The problem is often that the decision to carry out that particular intention turned out to be the wrong one. The story "Friendly Fire" discusses the tragic incidents in which soldiers on the same side of the war accidentally kill each other. Sometimes these tragedies are the result of action errors, which we discuss in chapter 3, and other times they occur because of an incorrect decision. In "Method to His Bratness" we see a detailed account of how and why decision errors sometimes occur, and what John McEnroe did to try to encourage them. Although many people associate "choking" in sports with poor performance at crunch time, a likely cause includes a change in the way decisions are made. Some of these are illustrated in the meltdowns described in "Choking Under Pressure." A rather different type of error is the focus of "Turn Right at the Next Gorilla," which describes the influence on performance of how we direct our visual attention.

What role did decision errors play in the death of Patrick Tillman?

Patrick Tillman was no ordinary American football player. He excelled at the game, playing as a defensive lineman for Arizona State University, then later as a professional for the Arizona Cardinals. At the height of his career, just months after the September 11 attack on the World Trade Center in New York, Tillman turned down a three-year contract offer from the Cardinals so that he could join the U.S. Army. He completed his basic training and eventually found himself in Afghanistan, fighting the Taliban. Patrick Tillman was killed there on April 22, 2004, but not by the Taliban; rather, he was killed by members of his own squadron.

U.S. Department of Defense officials refer to episodes in which an active engagement has occurred between units on the same side in terms of an oxymoron—they call it friendly fire. The Pentagon estimates that friendly fire accounted for 16 percent of all U.S. deaths in World War II, 14 percent in the Vietnam War, and 23 percent in the 1991 Persian Gulf War. Although each case of friendly fire has its own underlying causes, two general reasons for these tragedies account for a majority of the cases: (1) targeting errors, in which the target is correctly identified as the enemy and the fire inadvertently contacts a friendly target, and (2) identification errors, in which the fire is precise, but the target has been misidentified as the enemy.

Targeting errors may be caused by many factors that result in an action that was planned appropriately but did not end well. In many ways, targeting errors are similar to the unintended acceleration errors that were discussed in the "The Farmers' Market" in chapter 1. In these episodes, it is clear that the driver intended to contact the brake, but for whatever reason, the foot pressed the accelerator instead. Friendly fire targeting errors are similar— the intended target was identified correctly, but for whatever reason, the fire was misguided. The reasons the actions and movements become misguided are varied, and several of them are discussed later (e.g., in "The Gimme Putt" in chapter 3).

Identification errors are probably the more tragic of these two types that result in friendly fire, because the action was performed as intended, but the friendly target was incorrectly identified as the enemy. We make decisions of this general type many times each day. They are called binary decisions because we must decide between one of two available choices. Like the ones in combat (shoot/don't shoot), binary decisions are usually of the "yes or no" type. Do we have enough time to make a left-hand turn before the oncoming car arrives? Does the shadow on this X-ray indicate a cancerous growth, or is it just "noise"? Should the quarterback run with the football or throw it? Binary decisions are the result of an accumulation of information that leads a person to choose one option over another.

Although we make binary decisions like these all the time, very rarely are they made under conditions of heightened arousal such as the ones experienced by armed personnel in combat, and these conditions vastly increase the likelihood of making incorrect decisions. In the next story ("Method to His Bratness"), I discuss the binary decision-making process in more detail, including two fundamental reasons why errors occur.

A decision error ended the life of Patrick Tillman. His unit was on a mission and had split into two groups. Contact was lost between the groups, and when they finally met on a road in Afghanistan, one group mistook the other for the enemy and initiated gunfire.

SELF-DIRECTED LEARNING ACTIVITIES

1. Define the term *friendly fire* in your own words. What other terms could be used to describe this concept?

2. What is the difference between a targeting error and an identification error?

3. Find more information about Patrick Tillman's death. Why was an inspector general's report issued on the matters related to his death?

4. Describe the difference between targeting errors and identification errors when using a handheld communication device such as a smartphone (e.g., iPhone, BlackBerry). How might you conduct an experiment to separate the influence of screen and keyboard features on these two types of errors?

SUGGESTED READINGS

Friendly fire. (2009, May 14). In *Wikipedia*. http://en.wikipedia.org/wiki/friendly_fire.

Inspector General, U.S.D.O.D. (2007). *Review of matters related to the death of Corporal Patrick Tillman, U.S. Army*. Report # IPO2007E001.

Pat Tillman. (2009, May 14). In *Wikipedia*. http://en.wikipedia.org/wiki/pat_tillman.

Reason, J. (1990). *Human error*. Cambridge: Cambridge University Press.

Tillman, M., & Zacchino, N. (2008). *Boots on the ground by dusk: My tribute to Pat Tillman*. Emmaus, PA: Rodale Press.

U.S. Department of Defense. (2010, December 27). Department of defense dictionary. www.dtic.mil/doctrine/dod_dictionary.

Did John McEnroe's verbal abuse of line judges influence their decisions?

Former tennis star John McEnroe is remembered as much for his outbursts against umpires and line judges as he is for his seven Grand Slam victories. Also known as the Boy Wonder of Tennis and Superbrat, McEnroe is the only player ever to be disqualified from a Grand Slam event as a result of verbal abuse of officials (the 1990 Australian Open). Upon closer inspection, however, we see some method in his "bratness." Line judging in tennis requires the official to make an absolute judgment decision, which can result in two types of errors that have separate and unrelated causes. McEnroe's constant berating of umpires and line judges was his attempt to bias them toward making one of these errors in his favor.

So, what are these two types of errors, and how do they occur? In decision theory (also referred to as signal detection theory), these two errors occur because of the difference between what is actually true and what someone decides is true. In tennis, the ball is legally ruled to be in play when any part of it lands on or inside the lines that define the court. Figure 2.1 illustrates how often a ball would be called "out" as a function of where it landed relative to the boundary line on the court. Going along the horizontal axis from left to right illustrates how close the ball landed to the line—either well inside the line (on the left side of the axis) or well outside the line (on the right side of the horizontal axis). The dotted line in the figure illustrates a perfect world; in theory, a ball that lands outside the line is called "out" 100% of the time and a ball that lands inside the line is called "out" 0% of the time.

The dashed line in figure 2.1, however, represents reality—the calls that might be expected of a typical line judge. Note that the dotted and dashed lines overlap almost perfectly when the ball lands clearly in or clearly out, corresponding to the left and right extremes on the axis. However, they diverge as the ball lands closer and closer to the line. In reality, mistakes are made, and sometimes a ball that should be called "out" is not called "out," and vice versa. The gray area in the figure, where the dotted and dashed lines do not overlap, is, quite literally, that gray area in which the decision could have gone either way. It represents the difference between theory and reality.

Why are errors made when making simple decisions such as these? After all, the ball is either out or in, right? Decision theory suggests that we make decisions based on what we think we have seen. And what we think we have seen is based on an accumulation of sensory evidence—in this case, mostly

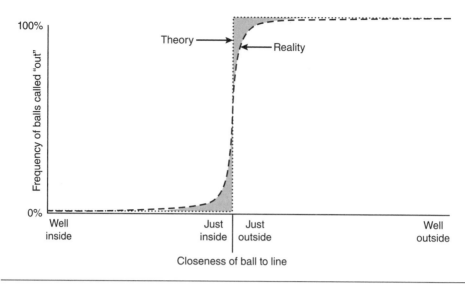

Figure 2.1 In theory, we should call all tennis shots that land outside the lines of the court "out." In reality, we call some shots that land inside the lines "out" and some that land outside "in."

visual evidence, which can be distorted. What we think we have seen may or may not be a faithful representation of reality. Let's think of the tennis line judge as a type of juror in a trial, who has to weigh the evidence provided by the lawyers and make a decision about whether the defendant is guilty or not guilty. In our case, the line judge is weighing the evidence accumulated through the senses and making a decision to call the ball "out" or "not out."

Decision theory states that people use accumulated sensory evidence to make these decisions. There is a subtle but important difference if you compare the horizontal axes in figures 2.1 and 2.2. In figure 2.1, the horizontal axis represents where the ball landed relative to the line. In

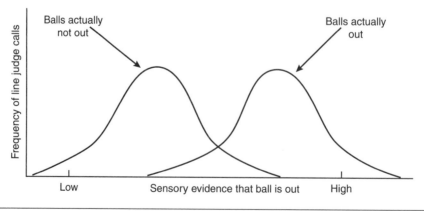

Figure 2.2 Signal detection theory applied to the task of judging whether or not a tennis shot has landed outside the lines of the court.

figure 2.2, going from left to right along the horizontal axis corresponds to increasingly stronger and stronger sensory evidence that the ball has landed outside the court. As in a court of law, the evidence must be sufficient to prove that the defendant is guilty; otherwise, the juror is instructed to find the defendant not guilty. The tennis line judge faces a similar situation. The perceptual evidence must be sufficient to conclude that the ball was out; otherwise, the ball should be called "not out."

The relative frequency of balls landing on the court with the associated amounts of sensory evidence is illustrated in the two "normal curves" presented in figure 2.3. These curves just represent the amount of accumulated sensory evidence—the line judge still has yet to rule on whether or not the evidence is sufficient to call the ball "out." The other important thing to note about this figure is that the perceptual evidence for "out" and "not out" is not always clear-cut; sometimes the evidence for an "out" call appears to have less strength than might be needed for a "not out" call. The spin that a ball takes after hitting the surface or the shading of light on a bright, sunny day might distort this visual information. This potential for confusion is represented in the graphs by the overlap of the two curves.

According to decision theory, the line judge establishes a criterion point along the horizontal axis that serves as a cutoff; beyond that criterion (to the right of it in figure 2.3), the judge will conclude that the ball was out. Failure to obtain sufficient perceptual evidence to rule that the ball was out will result in a "not out" call (i.e., to the left of the criterion point). The criterion point in figure 2.3 has been set at an arbitrary position along the horizontal axis that bisects both curves. This is a critically important detail about decision theory, because this bisection of both curves sets up the scenario in which the line judge could be correct for two reasons and incorrect for two reasons.

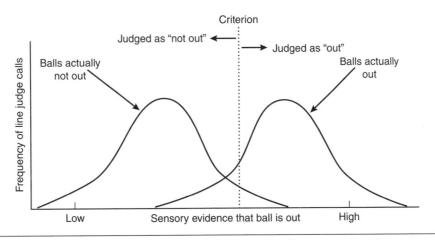

Figure 2.3 The tennis line judge uses the accumulated perceptual evidence to establish a criterion to make the line call.

The line judge is correct when the ball is correctly called "out" or "not out." The line judge is incorrect, of course, when a ball is called "not out" when, in fact, it was out, and called "out" when it was not out. The shaded region in figure 2.4 illustrates the latter error. This shaded region represents the area under the left curve, the distribution of "not out" balls that lies to the right of the criterion, and hence are ruled to be out. In making this error, the line judge has accumulated sufficient perceptual information to surpass the criterion point to make an "out" call. The other error is represented by the striped section in figure 2.4—a ball that is judged to be not out when in reality it was out. This region represents the area under the right curve that lies to the left of the criterion. In this instance, the judge has not accumulated enough perceptual information to reach the criterion to call the ball "out," even though, in fact, it was out.

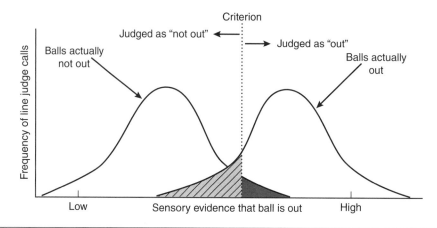

Figure 2.4 Balls that are judged to be out can sometimes result in errors if the ball was actually not outside the lines of the court (shaded area), and balls that are judged to be not out can sometimes result in errors if the ball was, in fact, outside the lines of the court (striped area).

There are two important things to know about these decision theory figures. One is that the degree to which the two distributions overlap will influence the potential for error. A line judge whose perceptual representations have considerable distortion (sometimes called neural "noise") will have more overlap of the two distributions. Perhaps this line judge had been out too late the night before and is feeling the aftereffects, or is just not highly skilled at the job. Regardless of where the criterion is set, this judge will make many errors of both kinds. On the other hand, a judge who is highly skilled and keenly focused might have very little overlap of the two distributions. This highly skilled judge is likely to make few errors of either type.

The second important thing to notice is that because line judges set the criterion point for accumulated sensory evidence, they can move the point to the left or to the right along the horizontal axis. This second source of errors—or, more specifically, the reason one type of error might be traded for another—is the likely reason John McEnroe yelled at line judges. He was trying to influence where they set this criterion. Nothing McEnroe could do would change how much the distributions were overlapped. But, because the criterion is under the control of the individual, he was probably trying to intimidate the judges into shifting their criteria so that there was less likelihood of an unfavorable call in the future. His strategy in berating the officials was a deliberate attempt to get them to shift their decision-making criteria so that any error, regardless of its type, would more frequently go in McEnroe's favor.

Postscript: Baseball Umpire Jim Joyce

Early in the 2010 baseball season, Detroit Tigers pitcher Armando Galarraga almost became the 21st pitcher in the history of Major League Baseball to throw a perfect game (defined as a game in which no player on the opposing team safely reaches base; every batter records an out in every plate appearance). In the ninth inning, with two outs recorded, the 27th player to bat in the game hit a ground ball to the infield and, even though the runner appeared to be out at first base to every person in the ballpark that day, he was inexplicably called safe by umpire Jim Joyce. Upon closer inspection, Joyce later admitted that he made the wrong decision—that, in fact, the runner had been out and that Galarraga should have made history for pitching a perfect game. How could this error occur at such a crucial point in the game?

In postgame interviews, a contrite Joyce admitted that he was well aware of potential history in the making and the importance of getting the call right. Joyce is widely known as one of the very best umpires in the game, and one who would be among the least likely to make a favorable call for one team or another, regardless of the situation. In other words, it is highly unlikely that the blown call was due to a shift in bias. Instead, the nature of the situation, perhaps enhanced by the building excitement among the home crowd, the players, and indeed, the umpires, likely caused a heightened anxiety and more overlap of the two call distributions (out and safe), thereby inflating the chances of making an error. As Joyce later admitted, "I missed it . . . this is a history call, and I kicked the (expletive deleted) out of it."

SELF-DIRECTED LEARNING ACTIVITIES

1. What specific technical terms are used to label the four outcomes of decision theory? Search the available literature to find these technical terms, and use them to label specific areas of figure 2.4.

2. Decision theory has been applied to many situations in which two-choice, or binary, decisions must be made. Use the graphs in figures 2.1 through 2.4 to explain how errors occur in a binary decision situation other than that of a tennis line judge.

3. For your application in question 2, suggest one factor that would shift the distributions closer together (more overlap) and one factor that would shift the distributions farther apart (less overlap).

4. For your application in question 2, suggest one factor that would shift the criterion to the left and one factor that would shift the criterion to the right. What impact would each of these shifts have on the expected frequency of each of the four outcomes?

NOTES

- Here is a good review of the research on decision theory, with many examples of using signal detection analyses in the determination of decisions:

   Swets, J.A., Dawes, R.M., & Monahan, J. (2000). Psychological science can improve diagnostic decisions. *Psychological Science in the Public Interest, 1,* 1-26.

- Of course, automated tennis machines that make line calls have removed much of the error in making the types of decisions described in this story.

- You can listen to the recorded postgame interview with umpire Jim Joyce online:

   www.tinyurl.com/jimjoyceinterview

SUGGESTED READINGS

Schmidt, R.A., & Lee, T.D. (2011). Human information processing. In *Motor control and learning: A behavioral emphasis* (5th ed., pp. 57-96) Champaign, IL: Human Kinetics.

Schwartz, L. Sportscentury biography: McEnroe was McNasty on and off the court, ESPN Classic, www.tinyurl.com/johnmcenroeespn.

What changes in information processing cause athletes such as Jean Van de Velde to fail under pressure?

The world of professional golf provides many examples of people who have been cruising toward victory, only to suffer a meltdown near the end. For instance, after three rounds of play, Greg Norman was leading the 1996 Masters golf tournament by six strokes, only to shoot 78 in the final round and lose by five strokes to Nick Faldo. Phil Mickelson blew a two-stroke lead in the final round of the 2006 U.S. Open with a bogie on the 17th hole, followed by a double bogie on the 18th due to a series of decision errors, leading him to reflect later, "I am such an idiot." Retief Goosen had locked up the 2001 U.S. Open, given two strokes to hole his ball from just 12 feet away. He three-putted. And Jean Van de Velde outdid them all during the 1999 British Open at Carnoustie by blowing a three-stroke lead on the final hole with a mind-numbing series of horrible

Figure 2.5 Jean Van de Velde considers whether or not to hit his ball out of a water hazard during the final hole at the 1999 British Open.

Michael Steele/PA Photos

decisions. For many people, these were actions of athletes who choked—when the pressure of the situation was raised, they failed.

But, what does it mean to choke, and in fact, did these highly skilled athletes really do so? The term would seem to imply that a particular instance of failed performance, when winning was on the line, was completely avoidable. Is that necessarily so? For example, suppose a basketball player who has an average success rate of 80 percent at the free throw line misses a foul shot with one second to go in the game. Is the player guilty of the label *choke*? Statistically, this player is expected to miss, on average, one free throw out of every five attempts. What would suggest that a miss in the final second of the game was anything either more than a statistically acceptable chance occurrence or different than any other time in the game?

According to researcher Sian Beilock, who studies these behaviors in various types of performance situations, choking is not simply an action performed in a skillful manner that results in an undesirable outcome. Rather, choking occurs when skilled athletes respond to pressure situations by altering the way they have learned to control their actions. Choking occurs for many reasons, many of them cognitive or strategic in origin, rather than simply as a result of suboptimal motor control.

Highly skilled performance, as attained by the very best athletes in every sport, is reached only after thousands and thousands of hours of practice. Researcher Anders Ericsson estimates that musicians and athletes generally do not experience their highest levels of expertise until they have accumulated at least 10,000 hours of practice. And not just any kind of practice will do—it must be structured specifically toward the attainment of skill, what Ericsson calls deliberate practice. This is the kind of practice that is mostly absent of fun and directed at the single, specific purpose of improving one's level of skill.

Many believe that the way experts control their actions is qualitatively different from the way nonexperts do. Theorists, such as Paul Fitts, suggested that the actions of experts possess a high level of automaticity because expertise allows the control of limb movements to be relegated to a nonconscious level. Because the expert athlete's or musician's movements are more automated, Fitts reasoned that they will have more spare attentional capacity to devote to less mundane issues, such as strategic concerns in sport or artistic expression in musical performance.

Anecdotally, musicians who perform at the highest levels of their profession describe experiences that support Fitts' theory. Stevie Ray Vaughan, one of the most highly regarded guitarists of the blues–rock genre, was apparently prone to this type of choking. He once said about his own playing, "When I play from my mind, I get into trouble." Fellow guitarist and friend Lonnie Mack reminisced that Vaughan reminded him not to get "too wrapped up in thinking and just letting it come out." When Stevie Ray did let it flow, however, the results were spectacular. Eric Clapton said that when Vaughan played at his best, he was an "open channel and music just flowed through him." These quotes are not unlike the ones you hear from many experts in other domains. To paraphrase the old Nike slogan, Don't think about it; just do it.

According to Beilock, the emergence of this nature of control also creates the potential for choking. After experts have attained a relatively automatic level of control, there remains a tendency to revert to thinking about how their movements are controlled (some call this skill-focused control), rather than just let it happen in a more automatic way.

In a recent putting study, Kristin Flegal and Michael Anderson revealed some clues about how choking might be induced by focusing on performing the skill. Groups of low-skilled and moderately skilled golfers in this experiment performed a series of putts, attempting to achieve a criterion of three consecutive successfully holed putts in a row. After taking their putts, half of the low-skilled golfers and half of the moderately skilled golfers described in as much detail as possible all of the actions involved in making the putts and where they had focused their attention during the putt. The remaining golfers in each skill group performed a control task in which they responded to unrelated questions. After these activities were completed, all subjects performed another set of putts, again attempting to achieve the criterion of three consecutively holed putts. The two subgroups that had performed the control task differed remarkably in the putts required to reach the criterion: as expected, the better golfers required fewer putts to reach the criterion (11 putts) than did the poorer golfers (22 putts). However, performance by the subgroups that described their putting focus in explicit detail was radically different. The moderately skilled golfers who had described their actions in detail required almost twice as many putts to reach the criterion (21 putts) as their control counterparts, whereas those in the low-skilled group needed roughly the same number of putts (20) as those in their control group.

Even though the participants in the Flegal and Anderson study were not experts, it became apparent that those in the higher-skilled group not only controlled their actions differently than those in the lower-skilled group but also suffered considerably when they changed their focus of attention. Such an explanation could account for a failure in performance in high-pressure situations when one changes to skill-focused attention. But, this explanation still leaves open the question about why people would change their focus of attention. What is it about high-pressure situations that lead people to think differently? This remains an issue of theoretical and practical interest on which much work still remains to be done.

An interesting postscript to the 1999 British Open is that, while Jean Van de Velde was coming apart during the final hole at Carnoustie, an on-air reporter made this comment: "He could have played the entire hole with his putter and gotten under 7." The implication was that removing the club selection process from Van de Velde at this time of great stress would have saved him from collapse. Revealing his classic self-deprecating sense of humor (and at the urging of his putter manufacturer, who filmed the event), Van de Velde agreed to return to Carnoustie to play the 18th hole again. On his third try he did indeed better his score, recording a 6 on the hole using only his putter for each shot.

SELF-DIRECTED LEARNING ACTIVITIES

1. Define the term *choke* in your own words.
2. Identify three other well-known cases in which a prominent athlete suffered a performance letdown at a critical stage late in the competition. Does each of these instances qualify for the label *choke* as you have defined it?
3. Identify a published experiment in which conditions of heightened anxiety (or pressure) have been induced. How were levels of anxiety induced in this research?
4. Summarize the findings of the experiment identified in question 3, and briefly propose a logical follow-up experiment.

NOTES

- Malcolm Gladwell's article in the *New Yorker* describes many more instances of choking in other sports, including details of Greg Norman's meltdown at the Masters:

   Gladwell, M. (2000, August 21 & 28). The art of failure: Why some people choke and others panic. *The New Yorker, 76* (24), 84-92.

- Stevie Ray Vaughan's comment about playing from his mind was reprinted in Schiller's *Zen page-a-day calendar 2008* (2006, Workman Publishing Company). Lonnie Mack and Eric Clapton's comments are from the Stevie Ray Vaughan and Double Trouble fan site ("What the Others Have Said About Stevie," www26.brinkster.com/jakapa/srv/quotes.htm).

- The following three videos document Jean Van de Velde's return to play the 18th hole at Carnoustie using only his putter:

   www.tinyurl.com/veldepart1 (part 1 of 3)

   www.tinyurl.com/veldepart2 (part 2 of 3)

   www.tinyurl.com/veldepart3 (part 3 of 3)

SUGGESTED READINGS

Beilock, S.L. (2010). *Choke: What the secrets of the brain reveal about getting it right when you have to.* New York: Free Press.

Beilock, S.L., & Gray, R. (2007). Why do athletes "choke" under pressure? In G. Tenenbaum & R.C. Eklund (Eds.), *Handbook of sport psychology* (3rd ed., pp. 425-444). Hoboken, NJ: Wiley.

Ericsson, K.A., Krampe, R.Th., & Tesch-Römer, C. (1993). The role of deliberate practice in the acquisition of expert performance. *Psychological Review, 100,* 363-406.

Fitts, P.M. (1964). Perceptual-motor skills learning. In A.W. Melton (Ed.), *Categories of human learning* (pp. 243-285). New York: Academic Press.

Flegal, K.E., & Anderson, M.C. (2008). Overthinking skilled motor performance: Or why those who teach can't do. *Psychonomic Bulletin & Review 15*, 927-932.

Gladwell, M. (2000, August 21 & 28). The art of failure: Why some people choke and others panic. *The New Yorker, 76* (24), 84-92.

TURN RIGHT AT THE NEXT GORILLA

What is inattention blindness, and what role does it play in common traffic accidents?

One of the more puzzling types of automobile accidents is called the looked-but-failed-to-see accident. A typical accident of this type occurs when a driver runs over a pedestrian or cyclist for no obvious or explicable reason. By all accounts, the victim could be seen in plain daylight, and the driver was not impaired in any way. In fact, the person or object is usually directly in the driver's line of sight. And yet, the driver failed to see it. Why?

What could be happening in these types of accidents is what researchers have termed inattention blindness, which, quite literally, means that simply thinking about something causes someone to be "blind" to certain aspects of the visual world. The cause of the blindness is a reduced capacity to perceive things around us when attention is directed to something specific in our environment. Researchers have conducted powerful demonstrations of inattention blindness, and their findings are quite astonishing.

I replicate one experiment in particular with my undergraduate class every year, and it never fails to amaze them. I have the students watch a recorded video clip. The clip is only about 30 seconds long and shows two teams of three people each passing a basketball back and forth. The teams are grouped closely together and are constantly moving, stopping only long enough to catch and pass the ball to the next member of the team. They weave in and out among each other, causing a lot of visual clutter in the scene, but you can always see the basketballs being passed back and forth. One team is dressed in jeans and white T-shirts, the other team, in jeans and black T-shirts. The task of the person watching the video is simply to count the number of passes made between the players dressed in white shirts.

After the video clip is over, I ask my students to report how many passes were made. Then I drop a bombshell with the following question: "Did you see the gorilla?" This is a fascinating video to show in my class because, as in the original experiment, typically about half of the students fail to see an actor dressed in a gorilla costume enter from the right and walk through the middle of the two teams passing the ball, stop, face the camera, pound her chest with her fists, and then walk off screen to the left (see figure 2.6). In fact, not only do my students typically not see the gorilla, but they don't believe that it actually happened until I show the video again (and even then, some believe that I have switched videos).

Research by Neisser and Becklen and later by Simons and Chabris discovered these results in their experiments using a variety of unusual events. One of the key findings to note, however, was that the gorilla was seen almost every time if the participant just watched the video and was not specifically asked to count the number of passes. Directing their attention to something specific in the video, in this case counting the passes among the players in white shirts, made people blind to the gorilla.

The research on inattention blindness provides important insight into the potential causes of looked-but-failed-to-see accidents. Driving in busy traffic and searching the visual environment for a specific object, such as a road sign, a building, an empty parking space, or a specific person walking along the sidewalk, compromise our capability to perceive information that either conflicts with or is neutral to the object of our search. We are not inattentive in general, but rather, our directed attention makes us unaware of objects in our visual field of which we would otherwise take note.

Attention-related blindness is also one of the staples that magicians depend on when performing card and coin tricks. The basic idea is to engage the audience in focusing on some action that is about to happen.

Figure 2.6   Would you miss seeing this gorilla walk through two groups of people passing basketballs?

Reprinted from D.J. Simons and C.F. Chabis, 1999, "Gorillas in our midst: Sustained inattentional blindness for dynamic events," *Perception* 28: 1059-1074. By permission of D.J. Simons and C.F. Chabis.

For example, the magician may say, "Pay very close attention to the card that Casandra has selected, and watch closely to where she has returned it to the deck." Meanwhile, as the audience is attending to the directed action, the magician has changed the deck of cards or slipped another card into his sleeve. Of course, all of this is done within full view of the audience, but the instruction to pay attention to Casandra has now made the audience blind to what the magician is doing.

Researchers have also demonstrated many other types of blindness that occur when we specifically direct our attention. Another fascinating study came from Simons' lab group that performed the gorilla experiment. In this study, one member of the research team plays a visitor to a university campus who stops a passing student to ask for directions. During the conversation, two other members of the research team, posing as workers carrying a large door, walk between the visitor and the student. While out of sight, the visitor asking for directions changes places with one of the workers carrying the door, who then continues the conversation with the unsuspecting mark. After the conversation was completed, fewer than half of the subjects who gave directions showed any awareness that the person to whom they were giving these directions had changed!

An important role of directed attention is to selectively perceive the world around us. That we actually misperceive things that would otherwise be quite obvious provides us with important insights about such things as looked-but-failed-to-see accidents and magic tricks. It is not that we do not see the cyclist or the sleight of hand, but rather that what we are aware of is largely determined by what we are intending to see.

SELF-DIRECTED LEARNING ACTIVITIES

1. Define the term *inattention blindness* in your own words.
2. Explain what the gorilla experiment demonstrates about looked-but-failed-to-see accidents and magic tricks.
3. What other experiments similar in concept to the gorilla experiment have been conducted in the literature? What methods did researchers use that were similar to those used in the gorilla study, and what methods were different?
4. How would you replicate the gorilla experiment using a different set of methods and stimuli than have been used in previous research?

NOTES

- A short demonstration of the gorilla clip from the Simons and Chabris (1999) experiment can be seen here:

    www.tinyurl.com/gorillaclip

- Simons and Chabris found that only 46 percent of their participants reported seeing the gorilla while counting the passes among the players dressed in white shirts. This number was higher when the participants were asked to count the passes among the players in black shirts (70 percent).

- Here is an interesting demonstration of change blindness in the context of a magic card trick:

    www.tinyurl.com/blindnesscolortrick

- A group of magicians has done scientific studies on magic and attention. Five of them were invited to present at a symposium on the magic of consciousness. Here is a reference to their scientific paper about attention and magic and a link to a number of their videos published online as supplements to the paper:

    Stephen L., Macknik, S.L., King, M., Randi, J., Robbins, A., Teller, J.T., & Martinez-Conde, S. (2008). Attention and awareness in stage magic: Turning tricks into research. *Nature Reviews: Neuroscience, 9,* 871-879.

    www.tinyurl.com/attentionresearch

- An interesting point is that, as in magic tricks, the gorilla in the inattention blindness experiment and the changed visitor in the door experiment are much more likely to be detected if a similar video is watched again. However, have a look at this video, posted on YouTube by Daniel Simons, for an interesting twist on this theme:

    www.tinyurl.com/gorillavariation

SUGGESTED READINGS

Chabris, C.F., & Simons, D.J. (2010). *The invisible gorilla: And other ways our intuitions deceive us*. New York: Crown.

Neisser, U., & Becklen, R. (1975). Selective looking: Attending to visually specified events. *Cognitive Psychology, 7,* 480-494.

Simons, D.J., & Chabris, C.F. (1999). Gorillas in our midst: Sustained inattentional blindness for dynamic events. *Perception, 28,* 1059-1074.

Simons, D.J., & Levin, D.T. (1998). Failure to detect changes to people in a real-world interaction. *Psychonomic Bulletin & Review*, 5, 644-649.

CHAPTER THREE

ACTION ERRORS

To this point we have considered errors that result from flawed perceptual processes and poor decisions. But even in the presence of good perception and decision making, our motor systems can still let us down. Three of the stories in this section are based on errors related to what is called the speed–accuracy trade-off. "The Calculator" discusses the pervasive role that Fitts' law continues to play in equipment design. Schmidt's law underlies the reason you should be very conservative in awarding a gimme putt to an opponent in golf ("The Gimme Putt"). "Pouring Coffee" invites you to consider how wise it would be to ask your mom to get out her finest white linen for an experiment. The chapter concludes with a motor control perspective on the often-humorous quotes of the Reverend William Archibald Spooner in "Is the Bean Dizzy?"

How can product designs accommodate Fitts' law?

LIBRARY, UNIVERSITY OF CHESTER

Have a look at the calculator illustrated in figure 3.1*a*. It is a pretty simple layout—not too many keys to get you confused, all are nicely labeled, the display is clear, and so on. But, from a motor control point of view, the layout suffers from a simple design error: all of the keys, regardless of their frequency of use, are the same size. Why does the 1/x key (which I have never used) need to be as large as the = (Enter) key, which I use on every calculation? In the calculator shown in figure 3.1*b*, I tripled the width of the enter key simply by removing a couple of keys that I never use. The new design should allow me to work faster with less chance of hitting the wrong key. The modification reflects an important concept in motor control: the speed–accuracy trade-off.

Paul Fitts was a pioneer in the study of motor control. His early work involved the study of errors made by pilots during World War II, and he was particularly interested in understanding the speed–accuracy trade-off in various situations. Fitts found that two components of aimed hand movements were primarily responsible for their speed and accuracy. One

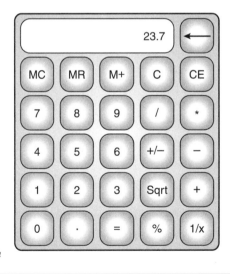
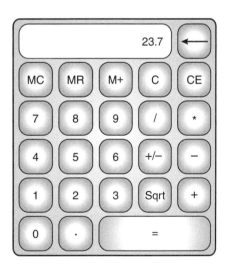

Figure 3.1 Compare these two calculators. In (*a*), all the keys are the same size. In (*b*), I have removed some keys that I use rarely and increased the size of the Enter key (which I use often). The rationale is based on Fitts' law.

component was the distance required for the hand to travel from its starting point to the target. The other component was the size of the target. In other words, Fitts studied movements that differed in terms of how far the hand needed to move and how much tolerance there was for missing the target once the hand got there. He studied these two components under various contrived experimental conditions that he could control and manipulate with precision, such as moving a penlike stylus back and forth between two rectangular targets, inserting pins into holes, and fitting washers onto pegs, taking extreme care to systematically vary the sizes of each item.

Fitts told his participants to try very hard never to miss the targets and examined how they altered their movement times to comply with that instruction. He found that movement time increased by a constant amount whenever the distance to move doubled or whenever the size of the target was reduced by half. In a typical Fitts-type experiment, the average speed to perform hand movements under various combinations of distance and size is usually plotted on a graph using average movement time along the ordinate (vertical axis). For the abscissa (horizontal axis), Fitts devised a clever measure of the combined difficulty of the task requirements using a logarithm to the base (2) of the distance and target size (because each successive data point represents an increase of twice the distance or half the size). Fitts referred to this measure as the index of difficulty, which is simply

$$ID = \log_2(2D/W)$$

in which ID refers to the index of difficulty, D is the distance to travel from the home position to the target (or from one target to another target), and W is the width of the target(s).

Experiments conducted by Fitts, and replicated many times since, revealed that movement time was a straightforward result of the effects of a task's index of difficulty. In fact, the results were so repeatable and generalizable that the finding has since become known as Fitts' law. Formally, Fitts' law is expressed as follows:

$$\text{Movement Time} = a + b\,(\text{ID})$$

This formula is nothing more than a variation of a simple linear equation ($y = a + bx$). In Fitts' law, y is replaced by movement time (MT); a is the expected movement time when $x = 0$ (e.g., in the tapping version of the Fitts' task this would be a situation in which the subject is tapping up and down with no endpoint accuracy requirement); b is the slope, or the constant increment in movement time whenever x is increased by one unit; and x is replaced by ID, which refers to the index of difficulty, as defined previously.

In the typical Fitts tapping task, a person is asked to move back and forth as fast as possible between two targets, stopping only long enough to tap down on a small metal plate, and continues this repetitive back-and-forth tapping for a period of time, such as 20 seconds. The number of taps is counted, and this value is then divided into 20 to calculate the average movement time per tap. Many trials are conducted to examine various permutations of the task that are made by varying the size of the targets and the distance between them. In the end, the data are summarized and illustrated as in the graph in figure 3.2.

The data represented by the squares and circles in the graph could be from two different people, or they could represent average group data from two different age groups, or they might represent data using two different computer input devices—say, moving a cursor on a screen with a mouse versus a finger touchpad. It really doesn't matter what the two sets of data points represent. Rather, the linear equations represented by the letters A and B in figure 3.2 indicate that A involves a slower system: system A has a slope of 50, and system B has a slope of 40. This simply means that whenever the index of task difficulty is increased by 1 (i.e., by doubling the distance or halving the target width), movement time is expected to increase by a constant amount that is equal to the slope (40 or 50 msec for B and A, respectively). Because the increase is larger for A than for B, system A must be slower than system B, because its processing speed requires more time for each additional increase in the ID.

The Fitts task is a specific version of the speed–accuracy trade-off because it places constraints on the user *not* to make an error. To comply with that requirement, the user must slow down when the task becomes more difficult. Note that A and B in the graph in figure 3.2 could also represent the calculators in figure 3.1. Because the Enter key for the calculator in

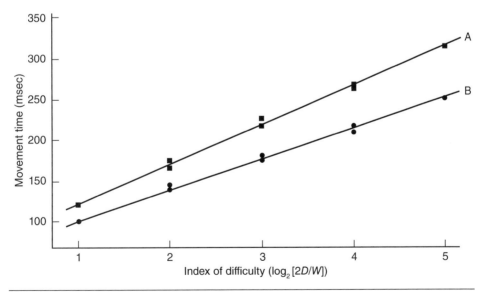

Figure 3.2 Sample graph from a Fitts-type experiment. The lines denoted by A and B could represent different people or systems. The steeper slope in line A denotes a slower processing system.

figure 3.1*a* is smaller than that in figure 3.1*b*, its operator must move slower than the operator using the calculator in figure 3.1*b* to maintain the same error rate.

So, given our knowledge of Fitts' law and how it affects the speed–accuracy trade-off in rapid aiming, could we use it to our advantage to enhance performance? In other words, can we *beat* Fitts' law? The calculator example given in figure 3.1 was a simple illustration. By removing a couple of infrequently used keys and increasing the size of the key used most often, I have dramatically improved performance by increasing the overall speed of making calculations while at the same time reducing the probability of making errors.

Other examples of beating Fitts' law are all around you. Here are two. The Apple Macintosh computer desktop has icons that that get larger as you approach them. This makes them faster to acquire and reduces the chance of clicking an unwanted icon and opening an application by mistake. The expanding sizes allow the user to move faster without increasing the error rate. An example of something that falls prey to Fitts' law is the typical computer drop-down menu. Compare the linear and circular (or pie) menus in figure 3.3. From the starting point denoted by the dot in each figure, you can see that the distance to reach each successive choice (from one to eight) gets progressively farther in the linear menu. However, with a central starting position in the circular (or pie) menu, each choice is equidistant. The pie menu and the expanding icons used on the Apple Macintosh provide nice illustrations of how the target size and distance components of Fitts' law can be overcome with a little ingenuity.

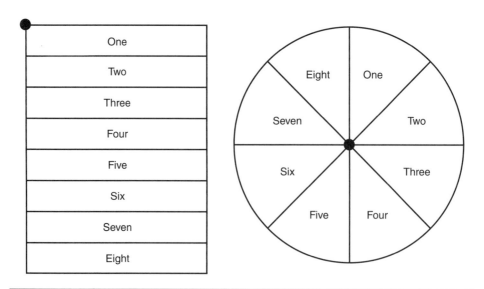

Figure 3.3   Circular (pie) drop-down menus reduce the speed of accessing a specific icon compared to linear menus. This is one way to beat Fitts' law.

SELF-DIRECTED LEARNING ACTIVITIES

1. Define *Fitts' law* in your own words.
2. There are several different ways in which speed and accuracy are traded in order to achieve a desired motor performance. Describe in your own words which specific version of the speed–accuracy trade-off is addressed in Fitts' law.
3. Describe another application (such as redesigning the calculator keypad or reshaping computer menus) in which you could use the understanding gained from Fitts' law to improve movement times, reduce aiming errors, or both.
4. Sketch combinations of targets and starting positions that correspond with IDs of 1, 2, 3, 4, and 5, according to Fitts' law (use appropriate combinations of target distance and width), and conduct a Fitts-type experiment, reporting the results as in figure 3.2.

NOTES

- Logarithms to the base 2 ($\log_2$) are not difficult to compute. For example, the $\log_2$ of 8 is 3—it is simply the number to which the base 2 must be raised to achieve the target number. In this case, 2 must be raised to the power of 3 to reach 8 ($2^3 = 8$).

- Take note in figure 3.2 that there are two squares and two circles for A and B corresponding to ID levels of 2, 3, and 4. For example, a task with a distance of 4 centimeters and a target size of 1 centimeter would have an ID of 3 because the $\log_2$ of ($2 \times 4 / 1$) is 3. However, another target combination in which the distance is twice as far (8 cm) but the target is also proportionally larger by the same amount (twice as wide—doubling the target width from 1 cm to 2 cm, in this case), would also have the same ID because the $\log_2$ of ($2 \times 8 / 2$) is also 3.

SUGGESTED READINGS

Fitts, P.M. (1954). The information capacity of the human motor system in controlling the amplitude of movement. *Journal of Experimental Psychology, 47,* 381-391.

Schmidt, R.A., & Lee, T.D. (2011). Principles of speed and accuracy. In *Motor control and learning: A behavioral emphasis* (5th ed., pp. 223-262) Champaign, IL: Human Kinetics.

Can Schmidt's law be used to predict the accuracy of golf putts?

A common gesture in friendly matches of golf is to concede an opponent's short putt when it is almost certain that it would be holed—the so-called gimme putt. This is a courtesy that speeds up play and saves the typical amateur player possible embarrassment. However, because even golf professionals are known to miss short putts, what length of putt would be reasonable to concede? The typical amateur golfer's odds are probably not much better than 50–50 of making a putt of 2 feet (61 cm) or more, even for a straight putt. Certainly, golfer error is a large contributing factor to this success rate. But golfers also miss short putts because of factors that are not under their control. For example, greens have debris such as dirt, small stones, indentations, and other imperfections that cause the ball to move off line and miss the hole. So, how much error in a missed putt is due to the golfer and how much is due to other factors?

Figure 3.4 illustrates some data that were published in a fascinating book by the Golf Society of Great Britain. The data represented by the circles were collected during the 1964 Dunlop Masters Tournament at Royal Birkdale in Great Britain, which featured some of the top professionals of the era. The graph illustrates putting success (putts made) from various distances. There was a rapid drop in putting success as the distance of the putt got farther and farther from the hole. Putts of lengths between 6 and 12 feet (1.8 and 3.2 m) were holed less than half the time, and putts beyond 18 feet (5.5 m) were made fewer than once in eight tries.

The square symbols in figure 3.4 represent the performance of a very precise putting machine that attempted putts at three distances from the hole (6, 20, and 60 ft, or 1.8, 6.1, and 18.3 m). Plotting the results of the putting machine against the results of the professional (human) golfers revealed dramatic differences. If the debris on the greens and other environmental factors were to account for all of the putting errors, then the putting machine's drop in performance as distance increased should have mirrored the golfers'. Instead, the findings indicate that human error contributed significantly to the error in missing putts, especially for putts beyond 6 feet. For instance, at a distance of 20 feet from the hole, the putting machine was holing half of its putts—a success rate that was about four times better than that of the average professional.

Some of this human error can be attributed to perception (e.g., misreading the break in the line of the putt) and decision making (e.g., striking the ball

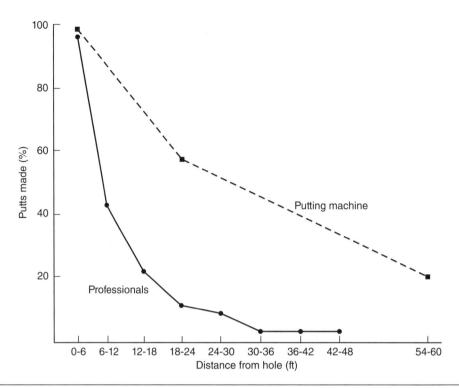

Figure 3.4 Comparison of the success of golf putts made from various distances by a human professional and a golf putting machine.
From data in Cochran & Stubbs 1968.

with too much force), but another important factor is related to a law of motor control—Schmidt's law. The importance of the law relates specifically to error variability—the dispersion of endpoints when we aim at a target (see the story "Cutting Wood and Missing Putts" in chapter 4 for more about variability). Schmidt's law for movements of short duration states that error variability is proportional to the force required to initiate the movement. When we make a brief movement to strike a target (a stroke of the ball, in this case), we do so with a certain amount of force. The force required to propel the ball to the hole is much less for short distances than for long distances. Because force and variability are proportional, we would therefore expect more variability for longer putts than for shorter putts.

An application of Schmidt's law to putting is illustrated in figure 3.5, which represents the error variability of three putts of different distances. In the top case (a putt of a short distance), there is relatively low variability at the point of contact because only a low amount of force is required. The pathway in gray illustrates the spread in possible outcomes that might be expected on, say, 95 percent of all putts. Because putts can be missed as a result of distance or direction errors (or both), the gray error bands in this figure illustrates possible error variability in both parameters. That is, some percentage of the putts would be expected to miss because of poor direction control, some proportion because of poor distance control, and some proportion because of both. Environmental factors notwithstanding, almost all of the short putts in 3.5*a* are expected to go in the hole.

The gray area in figure 3.5*b* represents a longer putt. Here, the variability at the point of impact will result in a wider dispersion of outcomes when the ball reaches the hole. In this example, the ball might be expected to go in the hole, say, on about one quarter of the putts attempted, and more misses would be expected as a result of both direction and distance control errors. Figure 3.5*c* represents the longest putt, which requires even more force and, thus, more force variability accumulated in the central nervous system at the point of impact. In this case, we expect that perhaps only one in eight putts might go in the hole.

When putting is viewed from the point of view of Schmidt's law, the task of the golfer on long putts is not necessarily to sink the ball on the first putt. Rather, the goal is to get the ball close enough on the first putt so that the second putt is no longer than, say, the gray area in 3.5*a*. Holes that take three (or more) putts to complete are usually caused by first putts that result in long second putts (as in 3.5*b* or 3.5*c*), which would then often require a third putt (or fourth or fifth).

We know from Fitts' law (see "The Calculator") that, for most tasks, we must slow down to be more accurate, or conversely, that speeding up will generally result in more errors. Fitts' law is a special application of the speed–accuracy trade-off that describes the effect on speed when accuracy is held constant and target size and distance to the target are covaried. Schmidt's law describes a related but different application of the speed–accuracy trade-off. Schmidt's law describes the relationship between force

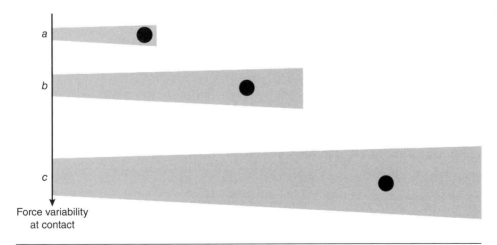

Figure 3.5 Putting variability increases with the length of the putt partially because of force variability principles (Schmidt's law).

and the variability in the error that is accumulated in the central nervous system prior to the initiation of movement. In essence, Schmidt's law states that the greater the force applied to a ballistic movement is, the greater the spread (or variability) of possible outcomes of those movements will be. A larger amount of force variability will result in movement outcome errors that increase both in the distance and direction variability of the movement.

The gimme putt is a friendly gesture that speeds up the pace of play on the golf course. Essentially, it is intended for the case illustrated in figure 3.5*a*, in which the golfer is highly unlikely to miss the putt. Unfortunately, for most amateur golfers, the force variability for even a very short putt is much higher than is illustrated in this figure, perhaps more like the case in figure 3.5*b*. The gimme putt is therefore a generous concession indeed!

SELF-DIRECTED LEARNING ACTIVITIES

1. Define *Schmidt's law* in your own words.
2. What research methods have been used to examine the relationship between force and outcome variability? What measures are used to define variability?
3. Apply Schmidt's law to another situation (other than golf putting) in which forces, and their variability, differ depending on the requirements of the task. What predictions could you make?
4. How would you conduct a research investigation designed to address the predictions you made in question 3?

NOTES

- The statement "95 percent of all putts" does not reflect an arbitrary number. According to statistical dispersion theory, one standard deviation unit is expected to account for 68 percent of all observed values, and two standard deviation units (the standard deviation multiplied by 2) is expected to account for 95 percent of all values. See "Public Opinion Polls" in chapter 4 for more on the rationale underlying this number.

SUGGESTED READINGS

Cochrane, A., & Stobbs, J. (1968). *Search for the perfect swing*. Chicago, IL: Triumph.

Schmidt, R.A., & Lee, T.D. (2011). Principles of speed and accuracy. In *Motor control and learning: A behavioral emphasis* (5th ed.) (pp. 223-262). Champaign, IL: Human Kinetics.

How does the information-processing rate create a speed–accuracy trade-off?

The next time you visit your mom or favorite aunt, ask her to take part in a little experiment. Set a coffee cup in the bottom of the kitchen sink and ask her to fill the cup right to the very top with strong, dark coffee. Ask her to do it as fast as possible, and, using your watch or phone, record the time it takes for her to pour the coffee. Then, ask her to spread out her finest white linen cloth on the table, and place the coffee cup on the linen. Again ask her to fill the cup to the very top with coffee as fast as possible and measure her time again. I can predict with great confidence that the time it takes to pour coffee into the cup when placed on the linen will be much longer than the time it takes to pour the coffee when the cup is in the sink. However, the likelihood that some coffee might have been spilled in the process is much greater in the sink than on the linen.

The coffee example is another demonstration of the speed–accuracy trade-off, which is a rather universal principle of not only motor control but also human behavior in general. The trade-off is that you run the risk of making more errors as you go faster, such as when I type too fast. To avoid making errors, I have to slow down. The trade-offs are that you can sacrifice speed for better accuracy, or sacrifice accuracy for faster speed.

Our ability to think and function requires that we perceive, process, and act on incoming sensations. The time it takes to process those sensations is the primary, rate-limiting factor in making decisions, be they movement-related decisions or otherwise. To avoid spilling coffee in our example, we need to be aware of a number of situations simultaneously, such as the current level of coffee in the cup, where the top edge of the cup is, and the rate at which we are pouring the coffee. These are sources of information that need to be processed—that is, detected and acted on. Assuming that we process information at a constant rate, it will take longer to process a greater amount of information than a lesser amount of information. The reason there is more information to be processed when pouring coffee into the cup quickly is that the level of the coffee is changing at a faster rate than when it is poured slowly.

Here is another example. Suppose someone were to offer you $100 to thread a needle, but stipulated that you had only one chance to pass the thread through the eye to win the money. How deliberate would you be in making that one attempt? The answer would probably depend on how badly you wanted the $100, but also on the size of the eye of the needle. Threading a needle requires that you continuously process the position of the leading edge of the thread relative to the tolerance for error, as defined by the size of the needle's eye. The smaller the tolerance for error is, the more information exists that needs to be processed. A large eye would require very little time to achieve success because the size of the thread compared to the size of the needle's eye creates a relatively large tolerance for error. Relatively little information needs to be processed, so we should be able to process it quickly without making an error. For a small eye, however, to thread the needle correctly on the first try, we need to move more slowly because the size of the thread compared to the needle's eye leaves little tolerance for error. Every millimeter or so that we move the thread closer to the needle eye requires that we update the relative position of the two, determine a measure of accuracy, and make changes to the thread's trajectory, if necessary. In other words, there is more information to be processed.

Fitts' law (see "The Calculator") was based on information theory and represents a specific type of speed–accuracy trade-off for movements to targets at varying distances and sizes. In one of the tasks that Fitts used for his research, he reasoned that the amount of information increased by one bit (or binary digit) whenever the distance of the target doubled or the size of the target was cut in half. Given a constant rate of human information processing, Fitts correctly predicted that movement time would increase by a constant amount for each increased *bit* of task difficulty. It is important to note, however, that Fitts required that errors be kept to a minimum. So, here is a specific type of the speed–accuracy trade-off in which movement speed must be slowed to maintain a constant error rate.

Hick's law, which I will discuss a little later (see "Red Light, Green Light" in chapter 5), is also grounded in information theory and explains the speed–accuracy trade-off in situations in which we must react as fast as possible to differing amounts of information. For Hick, the amount of information to be processed was defined in terms of the number of stimulus and response alternatives from which to choose. Reaction time increased by a constant amount whenever the number of alternative choices doubled. Like the trade-off in Fitts' law, the task was to make the correct response and avoid errors, so the subject had to slow down to respond correctly when more choices were available.

Schmidt's law (see "The Gimme Putt") addresses the speed–accuracy trade-off in a different way. For this work, Schmidt and his colleagues created targets of constant size and asked subjects to move varying distances at prescribed movement times, thereby creating different movement speeds. His finding that the spread of errors around the target increased by a constant amount relative to the speed of movement represented a variation of the same speed–accuracy relationship that Fitts had discovered, even though the type of trade-off was different—Schmidt varied movement speed and recorded the errors that resulted.

Researchers have examined many more types of trade-offs over the years, providing a fascinating basis for studying common elements of behavior in human decision making. Deciding whether to trade speed for accuracy, or vice versa, represents choices that we make hundreds of times every day; these decisions reflect the struggle over the goals we wish to achieve and the consequences we risk in striving to achieve those goals. I have a pretty good idea of what your mom would do when pouring coffee above her finest white linen.

SELF-DIRECTED LEARNING ACTIVITIES

1. Describe the speed–accuracy trade-off in your own words.

2. Describe how Fitts' law and Schmidt's law differ in terms of the speed–accuracy trade-off.

3. From the research literature, find what is meant by the temporal speed–accuracy trade-off. How does it differ from the speed–accuracy trade-off as described by Fitts' law and Schmidt's law?

4. In this story I asked you to conduct a little experiment involving coffee and your mother's best white linen. If your mother is like mine, that experiment would never actually happen. So, design another experiment that creates a similar trade-off as the coffee example does.

NOTES

- Fitts also used tasks in which people put pins into wells and put washers onto pegs, all of which could vary in size. The information to be processed in these tasks was related directly to the tolerance for correctness.

- The term *bit* stands for "binary digit," a measure of information that is directly proportional to the uncertainty in a task. Task information increases by one bit whenever uncertainty is doubled.

- In *Human Performance*, Fitts and Posner provide an amusing example of a speed–accuracy trade-off: the politician who tries to impress an audience by providing quick answers sometimes would be better off reflecting before answering.

- Apparently the speed–accuracy trade-off is not limited to humans; foraging behavior in bumblebees also reveals a strong speed–accuracy relation:

    Chittka, L., Dyer, A.G., Bock, F., & Dornhaus, A. (2003). Bees trade off foraging speed for accuracy. *Nature, 424,* 388.

SUGGESTED READINGS

Fitts, P.M., & Posner, M.I. (1967). *Human performance.* Belmont, CA: Brooks/Cole.

Schmidt, R.A., & Lee, T.D. (2011). Human information processing. In *Motor control and learning: A behavioral emphasis* (5th ed., pp. 57-96) Champaign, IL: Human Kinetics.

What do Spoonerisms reveal
about motor control?

The Reverend William Archibald Spooner served at Oxford University in England for over 60 years as a priest and a history professor and in various other capacities. But, perhaps his most noteworthy legacy will be for the things he said, not what he did. Following are some of the many quotes attributed directly to Spooner: at a wedding, "It is kisstomary to cuss the bride"; to a student, "You hissed my mystery lecture"; to another student, "You have tasted the whole worm"; and to a secretary, "Is the bean dizzy?" Indeed, the term now given to such oratory gaffes, *Spoonerisms*, is a tribute to the legend of Reverend Spooner.

A closer look at the nature of Spoonerisms provides some insight regarding speech and motor control in general. Take, for example, "You hissed my mystery lecture." Although the result is funny on one level (booing a confusing lecture), the error comes from a simple transposition of the first letters of two words, *h* and *m* (literally, "You *h*issed my *m*istory lecture" rather than "You *m*issed my *h*istory lecture"). A similar error resulted in Spooner asking a secretary, "Is the *b*ean *d*izzy?" rather than "Is the *d*ean *b*usy?"

Errors such as Spoonerisms reveal that we plan our words well in advance of speaking them. That is, you would not expect a person specifically to transpose *hissed* for *missed*, unless the person were planning in advance to use that *h* later in the sentence. For example, Spooner did not say, "You kissed my mystery lecture," because a word beginning with the letter *k* was not planned to be used later in the sentence. The "bean dizzy" example is also a clear case of mixing both the initial letters of the two words and their phonetic similarity. Another example, "You have tasted the whole worm," shows that the mixed words need not be consecutive words in the sentence; here the words *the whole* are correctly inserted between Spooner's attempt to say "wasted" and "term."

The idea that errors result from mistakes in action planning may seem like a commonsense view today; it fits well with many views of motor control, such as motor program theory. However, this way of conceptualizing Spoonerisms was a radical departure from the dominant theory of behaviorism that ruled much of the thinking in psychology during the first half of the 20th century. According to the behaviorist view, we create serial orders of behavior by stringing together sequences of discrete actions, such that the completion of one action becomes the stimulus for the production of the next in the series. Behaviorist methods such as shaping and chaining used various reinforcement techniques to train sequences of behaviors in experiments. The results of behaviorist techniques can readily be seen in the unnatural actions of trained animals, such as dancing bears and ball-balancing seals. According to the behaviorist view, a sequence of events is not planned in advance. Instead, the completion of one event in the chain becomes the stimulus to produce the next.

Karl Lashley, a physiological psychologist who conducted research during this dominant period of behaviorism, took a strong view against behaviorist theory, especially as it related to the performance of actions. Lashley argued instead that the brain creates behavior plans that allow a sequence of actions to be organized in advance and performed without the step-by-step, stimulus–response serial process proposed by behaviorism. Lashley's views laid the groundwork for motor program theories of movement control, which will be discussed in greater detail in part II (e.g., see "Antilock Brakes" in chapter 5 and "Forensic Motor Control" in chapter 7). Basically, a motor program is a sequence of behaviors that are planned in advance and then "run off" under the control of the program when triggered by the performer.

Spoonerisms represent one type of motor error in which the advance preparation of the sequence goes astray. Many other examples from speech and other forms of serial behaviors (such as typing *hte* instead of *the*) are common and have been the focus of researchers for many years. But few are as notorious as the mistakes made by Reverend Spooner.

SELF-DIRECTED LEARNING ACTIVITIES

1. Define *Spoonerism* in your own words.
2. What is behaviorism in the tradition of experimental psychology? Do some research if needed to find out what behaviorism suggests about (a) the production of movement, (b) the role of reinforcement in learning, and (c) the roles of cognition and information processing.
3. Keep a log (or diary) over a five-day period, and document all examples of substitution, transposition, and other Spoonerism-type errors you observe in speech and language (e.g., in typing).
4. Using your log of errors from question 3, combine errors into categories. Be creative when considering why and how two or more very different errors may have resulted from a similar fundamental process.

SUGGESTED READINGS

Bruce, D. (1994). Lashley and the problem of serial order. *American Psychologist, 49,* 93-103.

Dell, G.S. (1986). A spreading-activation theory of retrieval in sentence production. *Psychological Review, 93,* 283-321.

Lashley, K.S. (1951). The problem of serial order in behavior. In L.A. Jeffress (Ed.), *Cerebral mechanisms in behavior: The Hixon symposium* (pp. 112-136). New York: Wiley.

Miller, G.A., Galanter, E., & Pribram, K.H. (1960). *Plans and the structure of behavior*. New York: Holt, Rinehart & Winston.

Rosenbaum, D.A. (2009). *Human motor control* (2nd ed.). San Diego: Academic Press.

PART TWO

ADVENTURES IN PERCEPTION AND ACTION

Consider the simple act of closing our eyelids. We can close them and keep them closed if we are trying to go to sleep, to stop from seeing something distasteful, or just to give our eyes a rest. We can close our eyelids and pretend to be asleep if we want someone to think that we are asleep. We can close them partly to block out some light, and we can do so quickly or slowly. We can choose to close just one eyelid, perhaps in a seductive manner. We can alternate closing one and then the other. We blink frequently and involuntarily to keep our eyes moist and in response to stimulants. However, we can also be trained to blink involuntarily as a conditioned response to an unrelated stimulus. All of these examples involve the simple process of closing our eyes. And yet, such a seemingly simple process can be conducted in many different ways and with many different purposes. And not directly observable is the fact that eyelid closing can be achieved with a limitless number of combinations of muscle contractions, neural stimulations, and time–force properties.

Controlling our eyelids also has profound implications on what we see and don't see. Obviously, it is difficult to see anything when our eyelids are closed. But, how much information do we really miss during the brief time that our eyelids are closed during a blink or a wink? And does that loss of information have any influence at all on our visual perception of the world?

As we will see in the chapters in part II, perception and action are studied in many ways, using many investigative techniques. The stories are varied, but they all address our fascinating capability to move about in the world.

CHAPTER FOUR

FUN WITH NUMBERS

Our understanding of perception and action is grounded in research. Behavioral experiments are conducted to help us understand how we perceive and act. These experiments result in data—numbers and trends that illustrate how we perform motor skills. Because I discuss various types of numbers repeatedly in this part and the next one, let's begin with a few stories about the nature of data and some of the ways data are used to represent performance.

Former British Prime Minister Benjamin Disraeli was alleged to have said that there are "lies, damned lies, and statistics." So, what context could be more appropriate for a primer on statistics than politics? In the story "Public Opinion Polls" I try to demystify some of the jargon and fuddle-duddle that occur in the reporting of research data. The nature of constant and variable errors underlies "Cutting Wood and Missing Putts" and also explains why I have a separate stack of wood logs that are too big for my woodstove. One of our more prominent and widely accepted sport beliefs comes under fire in "The Hot Hand," thanks to a statistical analysis of the data.

PUBLIC OPINION POLLS

What do central tendency, variability, and statistical significance mean in the context of motor control research?

Have you ever wondered what the numbers mean when reporters announce the results of election campaign polls? For example, a reporter says that "Candidate X received an average support of 47 percent of the voters who were polled in the survey, candidate Y received an average of 21 percent of their support, and 32 percent of the voters surveyed have not yet made up their minds. These results are considered accurate within ± 4 percent, or 95 times out of 100." In a very few words, the reporter has managed to provide a lot of statistics, some that may be lost on the typical voter. Though they sound complicated, in fact these numbers are very simple. And, most important for our purposes, the statistics used in public opinion statements are the very same ones used in studies of perception and action.

The concept of a central tendency is implied by the term "average" as it relates to the support for each of the candidates. The concept of a statistical average is simple: These are just arithmetic averages, or means. If 258 voters were surveyed and 121 of them supported candidate X, then 121 / 258 = 46.9 percent and can be rounded up to 47 percent for the sake of simplicity. The statement "correct within ± 4 percent, or 95 times out of 100" requires a little more explanation. The implication here is that if 100 polls were conducted, each time polling a different sample of people, and all other factors were more or less equal (e.g., same date of the poll, same population from which the sample is taken), then the means reported would be approximately the same in at least 95 of these 100 polls (here *approximately* means within plus or minus 4 percent of the means that were reported in the original poll—that is, between 43 and 51 percent, for a reported mean of 47 percent). The pollsters recognize that their methods are not foolproof, however, and so they add the caveat that the poll could be wrong. They say that, by random chance, no more than 5 polls in 100 are likely to produce results that vary more than ± 4 percent from the means reported.

Most reports of motor control research use these same three basic types of numbers: measures of central tendency, or average (e.g., 47 percent), variability ($\pm$ 4 percent), and statistical significance (95 times out of 100). Let's demystify the last one first. Statistical significance means essentially that one researcher's discovery will be repeatable by other researchers under similar conditions at least 95 times out of 100 (a sort of gold standard in reporting statistics in this type of research). Sometimes researchers report that their findings were "not statistically significant." This simply means that the confidence in repeating any differences found in their results did not achieve this gold standard, and therefore any reported differences in the means should be viewed with extreme caution.

Measures of central tendency (such as the mean) and measures of variability (such as the standard deviation) are often reported together in motor control research reports. For example, if you wanted to know the average RT (reaction time) of a certain sprinter, you could download the results of, say, that athlete's last 10 races and compute the mean and standard deviation. The mean would simply be the statistical average of the reaction times in those 10 races (the sum of the 10 race RTs, divided by 10). The standard deviation is a little more complicated. It is the mean of the squared deviations of each individual RT relative to the athlete's mean RT (then expressed as the square root of that value). In simpler terms, the standard deviation is the average deviation of each of the individual RT values from the mean RT.

Knowledge about the mean and standard deviation is often useful when comparing performances. Suppose that over their last 10 races, sprinter A has a mean RT of 150 milliseconds (0.15 of a second) and a standard deviation of 10 milliseconds; and let's say that sprinter B has a mean of 140 milliseconds and a standard deviation of 30 milliseconds. From these data we know that, on average, sprinter B had a faster reaction time than sprinter A. However, sprinter A tends to be more consistent (less variability) than sprinter B, and therefore, for any single race, is more likely to have a reaction time closer to her average than will sprinter B.

When the individual numbers are distributed fairly regularly about the calculated average (i.e., what statisticians refer to as being normally distributed), the mean represents an appropriate central tendency for the group of numbers as a whole. But, this is not always the case because the mean is not always an unbiased (or appropriate) representation of central tendency. I will illustrate this idea using some findings from an actual sprint race.

The IAAF (International Association of Athletics Federation) World Indoor Athletics Championships are held every two years, and the winner of the 60-meter sprint is crowned the fastest person in the world. It is amazing to watch one of these races. Because the 60-meter distance is finished so quickly (the world record is less than 7 seconds for both men and women), a premium is placed on a fast reaction to the sound of the starter's gun (see "Jumping the Gun" in chapter 5). In many world championship races, in which only the very fastest runners represent their countries, it is very difficult to detect any differences among the runners in reacting to the sound of the gun. If this were always so, then the average reaction time for the field of athletes in any given race would be a good indicator of the individual RTs for each runner in the field.

But have a look at figure 4.1. These results occurred in a heat at the 1999 IAAF World Indoor Championships for the 60-meter sprint. The figure represents the RTs for each of the eight runners in the heat. Seven of the eight runners had RTs of 142 milliseconds or less. But, one runner, Maurice Greene of the United States, who was then (and still is) the world-record holder for the 60-meter race, got off to a terrible start with an RT (251 msec) that was more than a tenth of a second slower than every other runner in the race (although he still managed to finish second in the race). What I want you to notice in this figure is that seven of the eight runners in the race had an RT that was faster than the mean RT for the field (143 msec). How could a mean of 143 be representative of the entire field when seven of the eight runners had RTs less than the mean? This instance, in which one extreme score has a large effect on the mean, represents a case in which the mean is a poor (or unrepresentative) measure of central tendency, due to a nonnormal distribution of the individual scores. The median (127 msec), also plotted in figure 4.1, is a better measure of the heat's average because, as the middle number in an ordered series, it is hardly affected at all by a single extremely different (or outlier) score.

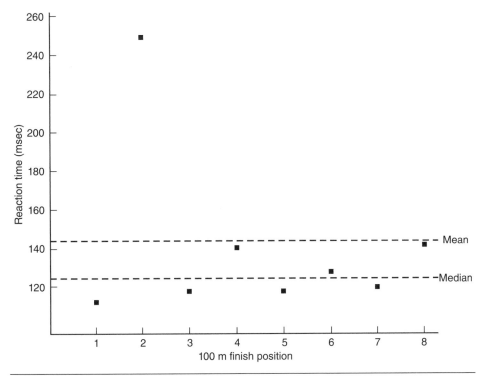

Figure 4.1 Reaction times for eight runners in heat 2 of the 1999 IAAF 60-meter men's sprint. Because of one runner's extremely long RT, the mean (143 msec) is higher than seven of the eight runners' RTs. In this case, the median (127 msec) is more representative of the true central tendency.
Data from www2.iaaf.org/wic99/results/index.asp.

Reading the findings of motor skills research in journals can be a daunting task because of all the numbers. In reality, however, most studies simply report measures of central tendency and variability, then provide some inferential statistics that suggest how repeatable their findings are likely to be. And the best part about the statistics reported in journal articles is that, unlike with politicians, you won't later feel guilty for having voted for them.

SELF-DIRECTED LEARNING ACTIVITIES

1. Define the terms *mean, standard deviation*, and *statistical significance* in your own words.
2. Find a published experiment that uses the preceding terms and interpret the results using your own language to describe the statistics.
3. Briefly describe two types of statistical tests that result in estimates of statistical significance.
4. Calculate the mean, median, and standard deviation for the following set of RTs: 125, 133, 177, 143, 161, 145, 201, 150, 166, 138.

NOTES

- World records for 60-meter sprint:
  - Men: Maurice Greene (United States): 6.39 seconds
  - Women: Irina Privalova (Russia): 6.92 seconds
- Results of previous IAAF competitions can be found at www.iaaf.org/history/index.html

SUGGESTED READINGS

Thomas, J.R., Nelson, J.K., & Silverman, S.J. (2011). *Research methods in physical activity* (6th ed.). Champaign, IL: Human Kinetics.

Cutting Wood and Missing Putts

How are constant error, variable error, and absolute error useful for understanding motor control?

Two things I like to do—cutting wood and golfing—remind me often of the importance of measures of central tendency and variability in motor control performance. For example, I use my chainsaw to cut up fallen trees to burn in the woodstove. Cutting logs into burnable lengths is not an exact science. In the middle of a Canadian winter, when the temperature is cold and plenty of snow blankets the ground, it is generally considered a good idea to keep moving. I do not take time to measure the lengths of the logs I saw; rather, I make a quick visual estimate and then start to make my cut. But, in doing so, I must remember two important things related to the mean and the standard deviation of the logs I cut. First, because our woodstove is only large enough to hold pieces of wood that are 50 centimeters (20 in.) or shorter, any pieces that are longer than that are useless. And second, wood is easier to stack when the pieces are all roughly of the same length. Essentially, these features remind me that the mean and standard deviation are both important; I must have a mean that is less than 50 centimeters and a standard deviation that is as small as possible.

When considering data in terms of a specific goal or standard, it is often better to express the mean and standard deviation in terms of error measures—in my case, relative to a goal wood length of 50 centimeters. For example, wood lengths of 45, 42, 48, 47, and 52 centimeters would be expressed as lengths that are −5, −8, −2, −3, and +2 centimeters, respectively, relative to my goal wood length of 50 centimeters. If we calculated the mean of these lengths of wood, then we could express the stack of wood as having either an average length of 46.8 centimeters, or the error scores as having a mean constant error of −3.2 centimeters. Having a negative constant error is good in this case, because the average piece of wood that I have cut will easily fit in the woodstove (i.e., the mean is less than 50 centimeters).

The careful reader will have noted, however, that even though my mean constant error is negative, there is still one block of wood that will not fit (the 52 cm log). Thus, by itself, the mean constant error score (−3.2 cm) is misleading, because it does not provide any indication of how many logs might not actually fit in the woodstove. Our measure of variability, the standard deviation, gives us some indication of this information. The measure of variability of these error scores (called the variable error) represents the deviation of the error score for each log relative to the mean constant error and is calculated in the same way as is a standard deviation. In this case, the variable error is 3.3 centimeters. In general, when I am cutting wood, I want to achieve a negative mean constant error with a variable error that is as small as possible.

Although constant error provides a useful heuristic measure of average performance in cutting wood with a chainsaw, it is a quite misleading measure of central tendency in another activity I like to do. Let's say that I have struck 10 golf putts—5 of these putts go past the hole by 5, 10, 15, 20, and 25 centimeters, respectively, and the other five putts come up short of the hole by equal amounts (–5, –10, –15, –20 and –25 cm). On average, by how much have I missed the hole with these putts? If you were to calculate the average as in the previous wood-cutting example (the sum of the 10 individual error scores, divided by 10) the answer would be a mean constant error of 0. In other words, my "average" putt ended up in the hole. However, we know that this answer surely must be wrong because none of the individual putts actually went in the hole. So, we must use a different way to express these error scores to avoid an answer that makes no sense.

The problem that we sometimes run into with constant error is that it provides a measure of average bias, the tendency to err in a specific way (e.g., by too much or too little; too far left versus too far right). In some cases a specific bias is desirable, such as the tendency to undercut a wood length of 50 centimeters so that all of my wood pieces fit in the woodstove. In the case of my putts that have no consistent bias, we are much better off using a measure of central tendency that removes the bias from each score prior to calculating the mean. Such a procedure is called using the absolute (unsigned) scores. Hence, this measure of central tendency is called the mean absolute error. Here, our measure of central tendency is the mean of the unsigned scores (5, 5, 10, 10, 15, 15, 20, 20, 25, 25), which is 15 centimeters. That is, the golf putts tended to miss the hole by an average of 15 centimeters. In this particular case, the mean absolute error score (15 cm from the hole) represents a more accurate picture of the entire set of individual scores than what is represented in the mean constant error (in the hole).

Averages are convenient ways to express how we tend to perform. But, numbers that represent central tendencies can be misleading if the tendency itself is not a strong one. Measures of variability are one way to identify the strength of a tendency. Depending on the context, different methods of calculating central tendencies may characterize the data in more representative ways.

SELF-DIRECTED LEARNING ACTIVITIES

1. Define *constant error*, *absolute error*, and *variable error* in your own words.

2. What do the terms *algebraic error* and *total error* (or Henry's E) refer to? How are they calculated, and how are they similar to the terms *constant error* and *absolute error*, respectively?

3. Look up and briefly describe a research investigation that uses at least two error measures. Why do you think the researchers used these measures in particular?

4. Conduct a brief study on yourself. Close your eyes and, using a pencil, draw five lines as close to 4 inches (10 cm) as possible, one below the previous one, without opening your eyes until you have drawn the fifth line. Measure and record the length of each line you drew; then calculate all of the error measures that have been discussed.

NOTES

• Here is a web-based standard deviation calculator:
  www.tinyurl.com/standarddeviationcalculator

SUGGESTED READINGS

Chapanis, A. (1951). Theory and methods for analyzing errors in man–machine systems. *Annals of the New York Academy of Sciences, 51,* 1179-1203.

Schmidt, R.A., & Lee, T.D. (2011). Methodology for studying motor performance. In *Motor control and learning: A behavioral emphasis* (5th ed., pp. 21-56). Champaign, IL: Human Kinetics.

THE HOT HAND

Do statistics support the existence of hot streaks in sports?

A common strategy in basketball is to pass the ball to the player who is currently on a roll, the person who has made all of his recent shots—the one with the "hot hand." According to the hot hand belief, of the five players on the court, the best player to take the next shot is the player who has successfully made most of his previous attempts. Many players, coaches, and fans insist that short streaks of success are common, and indeed, the data support their beliefs: streaks do occur rather frequently. But, the question of more importance here is this: Will a current hot streak accurately predict future success?

With the game on the line, would you rather have the person who is a 60 percent average shooter but who has missed her last four shots in a row take the shot, or the 40 percent average shooter who has made her last four in a row? There are three schools of thought on the issue, each with a different prediction about why one shooter would be preferred over the other.

The hot hand school of thought suggests that the 40 percent shooter who has made her last four in a row is "in the zone"—that mysterious (and mythical to some) mind–body place where confidence is high and performance is maximized. The answer to our little dilemma is simple from the hot hand perspective: regardless of who is the better shooter on average, give it to the person who is on a roll, the one with the hot hand.

The law of averages school of thought suggests just the opposite solution. The 60 percent shooter is normally successful on 6 out every 10 shots, whereas the 40 percent shooter normally hits only 4 out of every 10 shots. Because the 60 percent shooter has missed her last 4 shots, then the law of averages suggests that she will score on her next 6 shots (because she averages 6 out of 10, and has missed her last 4 shots, making the next 6 in a row will get her back to her average). At the very least, the law of averages suggests that she is certainly due to make a basket on her next shot. By the same reasoning, the 40 percent average shooter, having successfully made her last 4 in a row, is likely to miss her next 6 shots, or at the very least, she is due for a miss on her next shot. Therefore, the law of averages school of thought suggests giving the ball to the person who is most due to make a shot (or not give it to someone who is most due to miss), based on recent history combined with average success.

The statistical independence school of thought suggests that both of the preceding theories are wrong because of a fundamental flaw in logic. But first, let's consider some simple facts underlying this school of thought. Take a coin that is perfectly balanced and can be tossed without bias. That is to say, the probability of it landing with either the head or tail showing is equal (a probability of 50 percent, or $p = 0.50$). Tossing that coin repeatedly results in something called sequential independence. That is, the occurrence of a head or a tail on one coin toss will have no influence whatsoever on whether a head or a tail will show on the next toss. But streaks do occur in coin tossing. If you were to make a thousand tosses of a coin, you would likely find that a large number of streaks occurred, perhaps as many as 10 heads (or tails) in a row. But these are just chance occurrence streaks that are impossible to predict in advance, and they certainly do not change the likelihood that a head or tail will appear on the next coin toss.

Failure to understand this concept of sequential independence is the root cause of the gambler's fallacy—the mistaken belief that a long streak of repeat occurrences of independent events is more likely to be followed by a different event than another repetition of the same event. For example, a long run of reds on a casino's roulette wheel often will see an increase in the number of people placing bets on black because they believe that black is overdue. But, a fair roulette wheel, like a coin, has no memory; it doesn't know or care what happened on the previous spin, and every new spin is a completely independent event. The gambler's fallacy lies in attributing a sequential dependency probability value to a chance occurrence.

But basketball shooting is not a roulette wheel. To err is human, but to succeed is human as well. If the hot hand really does exist, then the implications for motor control theory are very important, because it suggests that our central nervous system exhibits periods of perceptual–motor behavior that is streaky. So, does the hot hand really exist?

The world of basketball hot hand believers was shaken when Thomas Gilovich and his colleagues published an influential paper in 1985. Gilovich and his colleagues examined performance data from several NBA teams in the early 1980s and found no evidence to support the existence of a hot hand. Indeed, the researchers found that short streaks of success were no more likely to occur than would be expected by chance alone. Sequential dependencies, in which a previous event influenced the outcome of a subsequent event, were absent in both the jump shot and free throw basketball data that they examined. It is important to note that they did not suggest that performance success was random, or that streaks of successful shots in a row did not occur. Rather, their claim was simply that the occurrence of a streak was no more likely than what might be expected by chance, much like the coin tossing occurrence of 10 heads in a row might be unpredictable yet still quite possible.

As expected, the publication of the Gilovich paper raised a number of eyebrows. Fans and commentators who followed the NBA, as well as other researchers, raised statistical and logistical arguments about the research and scrutinized the data and interpretations. One of the most persuasive arguments is that basketball data are insensitive to many factors that occur in a game, such as who is guarding the player, the length of time since a rest, the length of time after coming back from a rest (see "Shooting Two From the Line" in chapter 11), and the distance of the shot (see "The Gimme Putt" in chapter 3), each of which could have influenced the data Gilovich analyzed.

But the story doesn't end there. Evidence has now been found of hot hand streaks in sports such as bowling and horseshoes—sports that may be less prone than basketball to confounding factors that influence the continuance of streaks. The evidence is not yet complete on this topic, so a final answer remains to be determined. But, returning to our three schools of thought on who should take the shot with the game on the line, determining who is due based on the law of averages appears to be the worst predictor of any individual future performance. Sequential performances of skilled athletes may not be completely independent, and perhaps the nature of the sport plays a determining role in the hot hand. In the end, however, a player's level of skill is ultimately the best predictor of success for any single subsequent performance. The statistical independence school of thought provides the most reliable advice of all: Give the ball to your best shooter.

SELF-DIRECTED LEARNING ACTIVITIES

1. Explain the hot hand belief in your own words.
2. Explain the gambler's fallacy in your own words.
3. Pick a sport other than basketball and describe a situation in which a variety of predictions could be made about the next event based on the hot hand, law of averages, and statistical independence schools of thought.
4. Describe an experiment that you could perform that would test the predictions you made in question 3. Provide some basic details about how you would conduct the experiment, including information about the athletes you would try to recruit to participate.

SUGGESTED READINGS

Gilovich, T., Vallone, R., & Tversky, A. (1985). The hot hand in basketball: On the misperception of random sequences. *Cognitive Psychology, 17,* 295–314.

Oskarsson, A.T., Van Boven, L., McClelland, G.H., & Hastie R. (2009). What's next? Judging sequences of binary events. *Psychological Bulletin, 135,* 262-285.

Schilling, M.F. (2009). Does momentum exist in competitive volleyball? *Chance, 22,* 29-35.

CHAPTER FIVE

PERCEPTION IN ACTION

Perceiving our environment and reacting to it seem like some of the simplest, most basic of the actions that we perform each day. At least, that is what many people think when they talk about reactions and reaction time. However, the study of reaction time has many complexities, a few of which are captured in the story "Red Light, Green Light." But reaction times also have their limits. Just ask Linford Christie and Jon Drummond, who found out the hard way that there is a world of difference between anticipating the sound of the starter's pistol and reacting to it, as you will learn in "Jumping the Gun." Franklin Henry made a startling discovery regarding the role of a motor program in the length of the reaction time—a finding that anticipated its importance in braking technologies that had not even been used in cars when the research was published (see "Antilock Brakes"). Many people believe reaction time skills are critically important in sport. However, as we see in "Preventing Penalties and Batting Baseballs," any goalkeeper or batter who relies on reaction time to perform had better take up a different sport. As we saw in chapter 1, perceptual illusions can fool us into taking biased actions. In "Craps and Weighted Bats" I describe how we sometimes create our own illusions about how we control our movements.

What factors influence reaction time and its measurement?

Suppose you were driving down a busy neighborhood street and a child appeared from between parked cars to chase after a loose basketball. You would probably respond instinctively by jamming on the brakes as quickly and as hard as possible. Avoiding a tragic accident in this case would depend largely on your capacity to react quickly. In other words, you would want to respond with as small a reaction time as possible. But, even though reaction time represents the simplest and most basic voluntary motor response of all, the scientific study of it reveals that the reaction in this seemingly simple scenario is far more complex than we might expect. Let's begin with some simple ideas.

Consider the sprint start in a 100-meter race at the Olympic Games. After the starter asks the runners to take their positions in the starting blocks and everyone appears ready, the command "Set" is given, followed shortly thereafter by the sound of the starter's pistol, which begins the measurement of the sprinters' reaction times. Starting blocks are equipped with sensors that measure the sudden rise in force exerted against the block as the runners explode from their starting positions. This sudden rise in force is used to identify the end of the reaction time period (figure 5.1). The time between the firing of the starter's gun and the rise in force against the block

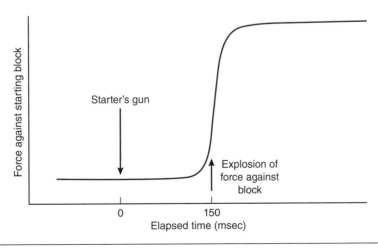

Figure 5.1 The measurement of reaction time in a sprint start. The sudden rise in force against the starting block signals the end of the reaction time.

defines the amount of time the runner needed to process the sound of the gun and initiate the sprint. In this way, reaction time is more strictly defined as the period between the sound of the starter's gun and the initiation of movement and does not really consider what happens after the race has begun.

So, let's reconsider our original issue, concerning the reaction time in responding to the child who has run onto the street. How would reaction time be measured here? Pushing on the brake pedal would actually combine reacting to the sight of the child *and* making a complete voluntary action to depress the brake pedal. Before the foot can touch the brake, though, it must leave the gas pedal. Therefore, one possibility for accurately measuring reaction time in this situation would be to assess the sudden release of pressure from the accelerator, thus signaling the initiation of the movement of the foot toward the brake. (The sudden drop in pressure on the accelerator would be similar to the sudden rise in force against the starting block discussed earlier in measuring the sprint start.) If we wanted to be even more precise, we could measure the sudden rise in activity of the muscles responsible for moving the foot off the accelerator, because they would show an increase in activity just fractions of a second before the foot actually left the accelerator. The point here is that measuring the time it takes to bring the car to a halt would include reaction time, but also the time contributed by many other factors, such as moving your foot quickly and forcefully to the brake, the environment (such as a slippery road), and the car itself (speed and mass). Reaction time would only contribute a small portion to the duration of this braking response.

Now let's consider another important property that influences the duration of a reaction time—what researchers call the amount of information that needs to be processed. Much of that information is contained in the visual signs and symbols that we respond to every day. My computer tells me when it is safe to unplug some hardware, when I should update my virus protection, and when I have a new e-mail in my inbox. Little symbols on my car's dash display that I can see through my steering wheel tell me things such as when it is time for an oil change (and many other things that make no sense to me at all, requiring me to look them up in that little book in the glove compartment). All of these signals differ in terms of the amount of information they convey and what they tell me to do.

We respond the quickest and most reliably to signals that are the simplest—the ones that suggest no choices in how we should respond. Take traffic signals, for instance. They tell us when it is safe to go or stay put and when pedestrians should walk or not walk. Some intersections use a very simple design to indicate information. The simplest signal contains just one light that may flash or stay on all the time. For example, some intersections use a flashing red light to indicate that a stop is required. But, because the light is conveying only one piece of information that never changes, there is really no decision to make—we just do what the light tells us to do.

A more complicated signal uses a two-light system. At a toll booth, for example, the red light indicates that you must stop and drop coins in the collection bin. The red light goes off and a green light comes on when the required amount has been received. The light tells you to keep your foot on the brake while the red light is on and not to remove it until the light changes from red to green. There is now a choice in what action to take. No decision needed to be made in the previous example of the flashing red light—you just did what the lone signal indicated that you should do. At the toll booth, however, you need to understand what the signal is (green or red), decide what it means (stay or go), and then act in an appropriate manner.

The common traffic intersection light is more complicated. The three-light system includes an amber light between the periods of green and red. The three-light system is an interesting one because two of the lights have definitive stimulus–response mappings: green means "go" and red means "stop" (or "don't go"), but what does the amber light tell you to do? The amber light is a warning signal that informs you that a red light is about to appear, and the change of the traffic signal from green to amber suggests that you need to instantaneously process all of the current traffic factors and make an appropriate response from one of two choices: either proceed through the intersection or stop before entering it. You use information at your discretion to make the decision based on various factors, such as your current speed, the distance from entering the intersection, road conditions, and your mental state. In a sense, the three-light traffic signal requires one of four possible responses: green means "go," red means "stop," and amber means "go or stop."

Some traffic lights have a fourth light, indicating a protected left turn. The fourth light might be a left-pointing arrow that then turns green, then amber, then red. If I am in the line of cars waiting to make a left turn, the choices about how to act have now become quite numerous. In other words, the traffic signal becomes more and more complex as the number of lights and responses to be made gets larger and larger.

Many researchers believe that uncertainty is the primary cause of complexity and equate the amount of information to be processed with the uncertainty about an event. The reaction time paradigm has been the most frequent scientific method used to study the effects of uncertainty on motor behavior. For example, suppose I asked you to rest your left middle finger on the A key on your keyboard, your left index finger on the S key, your right index finger on the K key, and your right middle finger on the L key. I can now manipulate the amount of information you are required to process by varying the choices you need to make.

Let's start simply by simulating the no-choice traffic light. With all four fingers resting on the keys as described, I tell you that a white box in the center of your computer screen will turn green for a brief moment every few seconds or so. You do not have to be concerned with having to make a choice about what the color of the box is and what finger to use to make the response; you simply have to press K when the box turns green (or more simply, when the box changes color, because it can only change from white to green). Your reaction time should be very fast.

Now let's make the task a little more complicated. Now the white box may turn either green or red. As before, I tell you to press K when the box turns green, but to press S when it turns red. You still don't have to be concerned with using the middle finger on either hand to make a response, but you do have to choose between index fingers, depending on the color to which the white box has changed. Your reaction time will be slower as a result of the decisions involved—detecting the color of the box and deciding which index finger to use to press a key.

I could then use four colors, with each of the four fingers mapped to respond to a specific color. But, you get the idea by now—reaction time will be even slower than before. More important, however, this experiment has demonstrated a fundamental feature of behavior—that the time required to process information (as measured by reaction time) is related directly to the amount of information to be processed. More precisely, the information to be processed includes reducing the uncertainty about what the stimulus color is and which finger is the appropriate one to use to make a key press response. In fact, this feature of behavior is so fundamental that it has been called a law of behavior, Hick's law, after the researcher who first applied information theory to explain why reaction times increased linearly every time the experimenter doubled the number of available choices.

I don't want to leave you with the impression that we respond to traffic signals as fast as possible. In fact, the traffic intersection is a good example of a situation in which we usually sacrifice speed to ensure that our decision is correct (also see "Pouring Coffee" in chapter 3). But the basic principle in understanding how to respond to traffic lights of varying complexity remains the same: the amount of information to process to respond appropriately is a direct result of the number of options available. Choice reaction time experiments nicely illustrate the concept that information is synonymous with the amount of uncertainty to resolve to make an informed decision.

SELF-DIRECTED LEARNING ACTIVITIES

1. Define *reaction time* in your own words.
2. Provide everyday life examples of reaction situations that involve one choice, two choices, three choices, and four or more choices.
3. Look up the empirical equation that defines Hick's law. What does each of the terms in the equation refer to in Hick's law?
4. Find a web-based demonstration of Hick's law and conduct an experiment in which you measure reaction time as a function of the number of stimulus–response alternatives. Plot and describe your data; then fit your data to the linear equation used in Hick's law.

NOTES

- Unfortunately, many drivers interpret the three-light system as follows: red means "stop," green means "go," and amber means "go faster."
- Here is a fun demonstration of the speed–accuracy trade-off in a reaction time task from BBC Science & Nature:

    www.tinyurl.com/speedaccuracy

SUGGESTED READINGS

Schmidt, R.A., & Lee, T.D. (2011). Human information processing. In *Motor control and learning: A behavioral emphasis* (5th ed., pp. 57-96) Champaign, IL: Human Kinetics.

How can a reaction be distinguished from an anticipation?

A subtle but important feature sets a true reaction apart from other types of situations in which we need to respond quickly to external events. A true reaction involves a response to an unanticipated event (or the unanticipated timing of an event). A good illustration of reacting is the sprint start or the sudden response to slam on the car brakes when a child has run into the street, as discussed in the previous story.

The goal of a sprint race is to determine who is the fastest runner. To make the sprint start as fair as possible, certain rules have been created to reduce the probability that a runner will get a head start by anticipating the starter's signal (i.e., jumping the gun). One rule charges an illegal (or false) start to a runner who has a reaction time of less than 100 milliseconds (one tenth of a second). The rule is in place because research suggests that hearing the sound of the gun and translating that information into the decision to run require time, and that time has been determined to be greater than 100 milliseconds. Therefore, the rule is that anyone with a sprint start reaction time of less than 100 milliseconds must certainly have anticipated the sound of the gun and initiated the response before the gun was fired.

The other rule that stresses the importance of reacting to and not anticipating the sound of the gun is the disqualification criterion. Prior to 2003, any sprinter who false started twice in a race was disqualified from further competition. A famous example was the British sprinter Linford Christie, whose dream of a repeat gold in the 1996 Olympics vanished when he was tagged with two false starts in the 100-meter finals. In the second of those false starts, Christie believed that he responded to the sound of the gun. However, his reaction time, as measured by the increased force applied to the block (see figure 5.1, p. 81), indicated a reaction time of less than 100 milliseconds.

With eight runners in a typical sprint race, however, the old rule allowed for up to eight false starts to the race before runners started to be ruled disqualified. After eight false starts, I'm sure the runners, the starter, and just about everyone watching the race would just like to see it finished. So the rules were changed in 2003 such that the entire field of racers was allowed only one false start. Now, after someone has committed a false start, the next person to jump the gun is disqualified. The application of this rule in 2003 World Championships is remembered well for the disqualification of

Figure 5.2   Jon Drummond at the 2003 World Championships after being disqualified in the 100-meter finals.
Philippe Millereau/DPPI/Icon SMI

the favorite, Jon Drummond, who was so upset with the ruling that he lay down on the track and refused to leave.

Reaction times are affected by a large number of factors, especially the properties of the stimulus. For example, a recent analysis of 100-meter and 110-meter hurdle races at the 2004 Olympic Games (men's and women's races) revealed that the runners in lane 1 achieved significantly faster reaction times than the runners in the other lanes (2-8). Since lane 1 was the closest to the starter, and therefore to the sound of the starter's pistol, the authors suggested that an unfair advantage was gained due to the properties of sound propagation. Another study revealed that the sound propagation effect on reaction time was magnified even more in the start of the 4x100-meter relay race, in which the distance from the starter to each of the lanes is increased dramatically compared to the sprint start race.

So, how valid is it to impose an absolute lower limit of 100 milliseconds on the start of a sprint race? Consider the following extreme example of how the stimulus properties affect reaction time in research conducted by Valls-Solé and his colleagues. They used a method in which subjects performed reaction responses to normal auditory sounds over a large number of trials. Then, on one particular trial, quite unexpectedly, an extremely loud acoustic stimulus was paired with the regular stimulus. The result was quite fascinating. Subjects produced the intended response with the precision of a regular reaction trial, but the response was initiated much faster, sometimes much less than 100 milliseconds faster, than the reaction times on the normal trials. Responses ranged from simple arm movements to whole-body movements (such as a sit-to-stand action). The argument the researchers offered for this result was that a motor program had been prepared voluntarily, but released involuntarily, using different neural pathways that were startled into action. My question is simply this: Is it possible for a sprinter, somehow, to be trained to be startled by the sound of the starter's gun? I am unaware of any research conducted on this question, but if this were possible, then the validity of imposing a 100-millisecond lower limit could be in question.

Regardless of the purpose of the false start rule, deciding the winner of a sprint race by including a reaction time component to the total time changes the interpretation of the skills of the winner. Instead of simply being the fastest runner, the winner of the race is the person who combines the best running *and* reacting times. For example, the medalists in the 60-meter finals at the 2006 IAAF World Indoor Championships in Moscow were Leonard Scott (6.50 sec), Andrey Yepishin (6.52 sec), and Terrence Trammell (6.54 sec). However, Trammell got off to a poor start, with a reaction time of 171 milliseconds. Scott's and Yepishin's reaction times were much faster (125 and 144 msec, respectively). Subtracting the reaction time from the final finish time reveals that, despite winning the bronze medal, Trammell had the fastest running time in the race (6.369 sec) (Scott and Yepishin were both at 6.376). So, who, rightfully, should have been crowned the world's fastest human—the fastest runner or the fastest reactor and runner?

This confusion between running fast and reacting quickly is not a problem in the sport of drag racing. The start signal for a drag race, in which pairs of cars race against each other, begins when the front wheels touch the starting line. Arriving at the starting line activates two pairs of preparation lights, followed by three amber staging lights on the so-called Christmas tree. Unlike the sprint start, in which the time between the "Set" command and the sound of the gun is varied and unpredictable, the illuminations of amber staging lights on the tree are separated by a constant amount of time (0.5 sec). The third amber light is followed very predictably by a green light. A perfect start would be a rapid acceleration of the car that is timed to begin at precisely the moment the green light appears. Essentially, this creates a reaction time of zero!

But, is it correct to call this a reaction time? Remember that a true reaction is a response made to an unpredictable external event (or unpredictable timing of the event). The sprinter who responds faster than 100 milliseconds is likely responding to her anticipation of the starter's gun. For the drag racer, the timing of the green light is perfectly predictable, and the skilled person is the one who can maximally coincide starting with its appearance. Such a skill is very different from reacting, however, because this involves primarily a temporal anticipation to a predictable external event rather than a reaction to an unpredictable event.

SELF-DIRECTED LEARNING ACTIVITIES

1. In your own words, define and differentiate between a reaction and an anticipation.
2. Aside from the loudness of an acoustic stimulus, name two other properties of the stimulus that would influence a person's reaction time.
3. Find a recent set of results for a World Championship sprint start, and separate the reaction times from the final times. Was the winner of the race the fastest runner or the fastest combined reactor and runner?
4. Suggest a method for determining the minimum allowable reaction time in a sprint race. How would your method ensure that the sprinter reacted to, rather than anticipated, the sound of the gun?

NOTES

- I use the term *unanticipated* in this story in the sense that we don't know exactly when or where the event that we respond to will happen. For example, in the sprint race, we know that the sound of the starter's gun will be heard at some point, but we don't know exactly when.
- See this site for a demonstration of the drag race Christmas tree and a chance to test your anticipation timing:

    www.howtodragrace.com

- Try this fun little experiment: www.mathsisfun.com/games/reaction-time.html. What effect did you experience that was mentioned in the story?

- For much more on sprint start reaction times, see this site:
    www.condellpark.com/kd/reactiontime.htm

SUGGESTED READINGS

Brown, A.M., Kenwell, Z.R., Maraj, B.K.V., & Collins, D.F. (2008). Go signal intensity influences the sprint start. *Medicine & Science in Sports & Exercise, 40,* 1144–1150.

Julin, A.L., & Dapena, J. (2003). Sprinters at the 1996 Olympic Games in Atlanta did not hear the starter's gun through the loudspeakers on the starting blocks. *New Studies in Athletics, 18,* 23-27.

Schmidt, R.A., & Lee, T.D. (2011). Human information processing. In *Motor control and learning: A behavioral emphasis* (5th ed., pp. 57-96) Champaign, IL: Human Kinetics.

Valls-Solé, J., Kumru, H., & Kofler, M. (2008). Interaction between startle and voluntary reactions in humans. *Experimental Brain Research, 187,* 497-507.

How does the complexity of a motor program influence reaction time?

Those of us who live in northern climates have to deal with icy road conditions for several months of the year. When first learning to drive, I was taught to respond to a skid on icy roads by pumping the brakes very rapidly instead of slamming and holding down the brake pedal. This is called cadence braking and takes both rapid foot movements and a keen presence of mind to be effective (not something that is easy to do when panicked by a car skidding on an icy road). Cadence braking is an effective method for cars with older styles of brakes, called drum, or disk, brakes—the kind of brakes that were installed on cars when I was learning to drive. Most cars now come equipped with an antilock braking system (ABS), which was developed to provide the pumping action automatically when the brake pedal is pressed hard. The ABS system was an advance in automotive technology that was created for a number of reasons, including one that the manufacturers never even considered.

Reaction time in braking, as we have discussed before, is the time that elapses between the appearance of an emergency signal and the initiation of the action to push the brake (see "Jumping the Gun"). The duration of a reaction time is affected by a number of factors, including one that is a little counterintuitive, discovered years ago by Franklin Henry. The participants in Henry's research responded to an auditory stimulus by making one of three types of actions that differed in complexity. In one portion of the experiment, the trials required that participants make only a simple hand withdrawal as soon as possible after the tone sounded. In another set of trials, participants had to complete two rapid movements as soon as possible after the hand withdrawal. Trials in the third portion of the experiment required four quick movements in immediate succession after the initial hand withdrawal response to the tone. Henry found that the reaction time for each of the successively more complex movements was a little bit longer: the second action resulted in a reaction time that was 23 percent longer than the reaction time in the simple hand withdrawal response trials, and the third action was 31 percent longer than the hand withdrawal response.

Some might think that these results are not surprising because it should take more time to complete a more complicated response. However, remember that reaction time is measured only as the time it takes to initiate the response. Because all three actions required the same hand withdrawal at the start, the measurement of the reaction time period was complete before any other movements were required. Therefore, the differences in the observed reaction times must have reflected differences in the latency period to get the response started, with more complex actions producing longer reaction time latencies.

It is interesting to note that Henry's work was conducted back in the late 1950s and early 1960s, when the idea of using computers as analogies to explain human cognition (i.e., the information processing model) was still in its infancy. His explanation for these effects relied on the analogy of a computer program; Henry called it a motor program. The idea was that learned, rapid movements are stored as a program in memory, which takes time to load when retrieved from memory. Henry's argument was that the latency to retrieve the program, here measured as reaction time, corresponded directly with the complexity of the response: the more complicated the required movement was, the longer the latency to load and initiate its motor program.

Henry's research has since been replicated many times by researchers working in different laboratories and using different types of actions with various response complexities. One of the experiments that more directly approximates the task of pumping the brakes of a car was reported by Sternberg and his colleagues. Participants in this experiment were asked to speak simple phrases as soon as possible after a signal was provided, such as *two-three-four-five-six*. As with Henry's research, the participants were well aware of the phrase they were to speak, so response uncertainty was not a factor in any of the results (see "Jumping the Gun"). Sternberg found that the time it took to begin to say *two-three-four-five-six* was almost 20 percent longer than the time it took to begin to say *two*. In the case of the participants in the Sternberg study, each word added to the phrase increased the complexity of the response and contributed about another 4 percent to the reaction time latency.

So, let's consider these findings in the context of braking a car on a slippery road. For cars equipped with the kind of brakes used when I learned to drive, the appropriate response is a preprogrammed rapid pumping on the pedal—say, as many as 10 rapid bursts of force on the brake pedal. For cars now equipped with ABS brakes, the response is simply a single, forceful depressing of the pedal. It stands as a clear prediction from the research of Franklin Henry, Sternberg and his colleagues, and many others that the time to initiate a single braking action using ABS brakes should be shorter than the time to initiate a cadence braking response using a drum, or disk, brake system. The unexpected advantage in ABS technology in automobiles was not just a more effective braking system but also one that is likely initiated faster in an emergency situation than the older system.

SELF-DIRECTED LEARNING ACTIVITIES

1. Define the term *motor program* in your own words.
2. Research what other factors specifically related to the action required have been found to influence reaction time.
3. Given what you found in question 2, suggest two other differences between a cadence braking action and an ABS braking action that might also influence the reaction time latency.
4. Create a methodology for an experiment in which you compare the reaction time to initiate a cadence brake response to that to initiate an ABS brake response.

NOTES

- Young and Stanton provide a good summary of other factors that affect brake reaction time:

  Young, M.S., & Stanton, N.A. (2007). Back to the future: Brake reaction times for manual and automated vehicles. *Ergonomics, 50,* 46-58.

SUGGESTED READINGS

Christina, R.W. (1992). Unraveling the mystery of the response complexity effect in skilled movements. *Research Quarterly for Exercise and Sport, 63,* 218-230.

Henry, F.M., & Rogers, D.E. (1960). Increased response latency for complicated movements and a "memory drum" theory of neuromotor reaction. *Research Quarterly, 31,* 448-458.

Schmidt, R.A., & Lee, T.D. (2011). Human information processing. In *Motor control and learning: A behavioral emphasis* (5th ed., pp. 57-96) Champaign, IL: Human Kinetics.

Sternberg, S., Monsell, S., Knoll, R.L., & Wright, C.E. (1978). The latency and duration of rapid movement sequences: Comparisons of speech and typewriting. In G.E. Stelmach (Ed.), *Information processing in motor control and learning* (pp. 117-152). New York: Academic Press.

How do athletes use temporal and spatial anticipation?

The goalkeeper in soccer is responsible for defending a goal that is enormous: 8 yards (7.3 m) wide and 2.6 yards (2.4 m) high. In a penalty kick situation, the player who is taking the shot has a free kick of the ball from a distance of only 12 yards (11 m) from the goal line. The closeness of the player taking the kick to a goal of such size makes it seem as though stopping the ball is virtually impossible. And yet, skilled goalkeepers are successful at stopping about one out of every four penalty kicks. How do they do it?

Unlike in the situations discussed in the preceding stories, reacting after the ball has been kicked is unlikely to be a successful strategy in soccer, given the time it would take to respond appropriately (reaction time) and then move into position to stop the ball. If the goalkeeper were to react to the direction in which the player has struck the ball, successfully defending the goal would be unlikely, if not impossible. Instead, the goalkeeper must anticipate the spot to which the ball will be kicked and begin moving toward that spot before the kicker actually strikes the ball. This type of anticipation is similar to the temporal anticipation seen in the drag race start (i.e., an action is made that uses predictable information provided by some external event). For the drag racer, the Christmas tree provided information that facilitated temporal anticipation (see "Jumping the Gun"). Although temporal anticipation is of some importance for the soccer goalkeeper, the more critical matter is being at a certain spot in front of the goal to block the shot when the ball arrives. This requires spatial anticipation; the goalkeeper needs to predict where the ball will be kicked.

How does the goalkeeper know where to dive before the ball is struck? If the goalkeeper knows something about the kicker's history or tendencies in penalty kicks, then an educated guess might be better than nothing at all. However, researchers have found that skilled goalkeepers use more than memory and guesswork to make these spatial anticipations. They see specific information as the kicker approaches the ball, despite the kicker's attempt to disguise that information. Studies by researcher Geert Savelsbergh and his colleagues used eye movement recordings to reveal that expert goalkeepers rely on visual cues provided by the kicker to anticipate where the ball will go. The cues detected by experts are more dependable and revealing than the cues used by novice or less skilled goalkeepers. As the kicker starts the initial approach to the ball, the expert goalkeeper tends to focus on the kicker's face, perhaps with the hope that the direction of gaze might give away the intended location of the shot. As the kicker comes closer to the ball, the skilled goalkeeper switches the focus of visual gaze to the kicker's lower body. In contrast, novices tend to be much less focused in their visual search and often look at the upper torso during the entire kick.

The information about the probable intended location of the shot, extracted during the run-up and before ball contact, allows the skilled goalkeeper to predict with some reliability where to dive to block the ball. Of course, this does not guarantee that the goalkeeper will actually stop the ball once there, but at least she has a better chance for success than she would have if she waited until the kick or merely guessed.

Extracting information to predict an object's temporal occurrence is critical for the drag racer, and information that predicts an object's spatial occurrence is of utmost importance to the soccer goalkeeper. Having to pick up on both sources of information is perhaps why professional baseball players are rewarded with multimillion-dollar contracts for achieving success in only a third of their trips to the plate!

A few numbers about baseball batting reveal why the task is considered so difficult to perform well. Although the pitcher starts his windup just over 60 feet (18 m) from the batter, by the time he finally releases the ball, the pitcher's hand may be only 55 feet (16.8 m) or so away from the plate. It is not uncommon for major-league pitchers to throw over 90 miles per hour (145 km/h), and some have been clocked at over 100 miles per hour (161 km/h). Although these numbers sound impressive, they are even more astounding when expressed in time. A relatively pedestrian 80-miles-per-hour (129 km/h) fastball takes just over half a second to reach the plate (517 msec), and a 100-miles-per-hour fastball leaves the pitcher's hand and arrives at the plate in just over four tenths of a second (413 msec). Hubbard and Seng's early research with college baseball batters found that they needed about 160 milliseconds to get the bat from the first motion of the swing into the hitting zone (above the plate). So, given all of these time constraints, how long does a batter have to make the decision of whether or not to swing at the pitch?

Let's assume for the moment that a batter will decide to swing at a pitch that is in the strike zone, and will decide not to swing at a pitch that is out of the strike zone. And let's also assume, for now, that the batter is reacting to the information contained in the ball flight. So, after the batter has reacted with a decision to swing, he must factor in the time it will take for the bat to arrive in the hitting zone (160 msec). Simple subtraction tells us that for an 80-miles-per-hour (129 km/h) pitch, the average batter has 517 − 160 = 357 milliseconds to decide whether or not to swing the bat. For the 100-miles-per-hour (161 km/h) pitch, that decision time is reduced to about 253 milliseconds. In all, that seems like a lot of time to make the decision (consider that a sprinter typically reacts to the sound of the starter's gun in 150 msec or so).

But, there are some complications here. First, the batter is not responding to a sound but rather to something he is seeing, and reaction times to visual information are typically slower than reaction times to sound. Second, coinciding the spatial aim of the bat requires that the batter accurately predict where the ball will be when it arrives in the area near the plate. Therefore, the longer the batter gets to see the flight of the ball, the better the prediction should be. And that is assuming that the flight of the ball is predictable. Pitchers have an arsenal of skills to increase the difficulty of predicting where the ball will be as it crosses the plate. The last thing major-league pitchers want to do is throw a ball that goes straight. Instead, they use various finger grips and throwing motions to change the ball's direction during its flight. And to complicate things even more for the batter, the savvy pitcher changes speed from pitch to pitch, thereby increasing the temporal anticipation complexity of hitting.

So, what strategies does a batter use to improve the likelihood of colliding the bat with the ball? Like expert soccer goalkeepers, skilled baseball batters search for cues from the pitcher, before the ball is released, that might tip them off about the nature of the pitch. Being able to visually detect these tip-off cues is mandatory for achieving some measure of success (and money). For example, the location of the ball in the pitcher's hand can give the batter some indication of the type of pitch being thrown. A ball tucked between the index and middle fingers could be a tip-off that the pitcher is going to throw a split-fingered fastball. If the ball is held deep in the palm of the hand, or grasped between the thumb and index finger, then a slower-than-normal pitch (called a changeup) is likely on the way. Of course, the pitcher will try to hide this information by keeping the throwing hand out of sight from the batter for as long as possible. So, the skilled batter must try to pick up this information as early as possible during the pitch.

As with the soccer goalkeeper, if the batter must react to the ball as it arrives near the plate, then the odds of success are very poor. But these odds improve dramatically when the batter can use temporal and spatial anticipation. Perhaps this explains why baseball players frequently remark, after a particularly good day of batting, that they were "seeing the ball well today."

SELF-DIRECTED LEARNING ACTIVITIES

1. Define *spatial anticipation* and *temporal anticipation* in your own words.

2. Given the numbers presented in the story for the durations to deliver pitches of different speeds and bat swing times, calculate how much time a batter would have to make a decision for a 90-miles-per-hour (145 km/h) fastball and a 140-millisecond bat swing duration.

3. Do some research if needed and identify two types of occlusion methods that have been used in research to examine the nature of perceptual expertise in sport.

4. Pick a sport task, other than goalkeeping and batting, in which spatial and temporal anticipation serve an important role, and speculate on the nature of advanced search clues used by skilled athletes.

NOTES

- Here is a pitching speed calculator:
  www.tinyurl.com/pitchspeed
- When I pitched for the Dundas Chiefs senior baseball team, my 68-miles-per-hour (109 km/h) fastball took about six tenths of a second to arrive at the plate. Batters could yawn during my pitches and still have plenty of time to hit the ball . . . and hit it hard . . . to places far, far away.

SUGGESTED READINGS

Hubbard, A.W., & Seng, C.N. (1954). Visual movements of batters. *Research Quarterly, 25,* 42-57.

Savelsbergh, G.J.P., Williams, A.M., Van der Kamp, J., & Ward, P. (2002). Visual search, anticipation and expertise in soccer goalkeepers. *Journal of Sports Sciences, 20,* 279-287.

Schmidt, R.A., & Lee, T.D. (2011). Central contributions to motor control. In *Motor control and learning: A behavioral emphasis* (5th ed., pp. 177-222) Champaign, IL: Human Kinetics.

What role do perceptual illusions play in sport performance?

In chapter 1 of this book, you read about various illusions that occur when our visual system predisposes us to certain expectations (see "The Magnetic Hill" in chapter 1). A visual illusion in the magnetic hill makes us feel as though our car is coasting uphill. The visual conflict between vision and audition in the McGurk effect makes us hear something that isn't there. But visual perceptions and expectations are not the only ways we are misled. Illusions of performance are caused by many other factors too.

One of the more curious things you might see on TV occurs during professional golf events. Watch the golfer's reaction after striking the ball off the tee box area. If the TV camera stays focused on the golfer rather than the ball, you will likely know the ball's flight direction simply by watching how the golfer leans. If the ball is going to the right of the golfer's intended target, she will likely lean to the left. If the ball is going left of the target, she will likely lean to the right. But, the golfer no longer has any control over where the ball will go after it has left the club face. So, why behave like that?

As it turns out, this type of behavior is not peculiar to golfers. James Henslin described a similar phenomenon many years ago regarding the behavior of taxi cab drivers, who often spent their free time playing craps. The game of craps is played with two dice, and the goal is simple. If the total of the two dice on the first roll is 7 or 11, then the player scores a "natural" and instantly wins the bet. If the total on the first roll is 2, 3, or 12, then the person has rolled a "craps" and instantly loses the bet. All other totals (4, 5, 6, 8, 9, 10) achieved on the first roll are considered to set the "point," after which the player rolls the dice again and again until one of two totals occur—a repeat of the point or a 7. The player wins if the point is rolled again but loses if a 7 is rolled first.

It is in this latter situation, when the cab drivers were trying to achieve the point, that Henslin noted something similar to the behavior of professional golfers. He observed that the cab drivers tended to throw the dice harder when trying to achieve a point that was greater than 7 (an 8, 9, or 10) and to throw the dice more softly when trying to achieve a lower sum (4, 5, or 6). The cab drivers also performed ritualistic activities such as talking to the dice before rolling them or snapping their fingers after the roll, just before the dice settled. Although the outcome of rolled dice was entirely due to chance, these highly experienced craps players firmly believed that their behaviors before, during, and after the roll had an influence on the outcome of the dice. Ellen Langer later called this type of behavior an illusion of control—the tendency to take credit for or apply reasoning to outcomes that are beyond the performer's control.

Some baseball players use illusions in a very purposeful manner. The term *kinesthetic aftereffect* refers to the sensations that remain after an action has been completed—for example, after a heavy object has been lifted. Try holding a 10-pound (4.5 kg) bag of sugar in your outstretched hand for a period of time. After the weight has been removed, your arm will feel lighter for a short period of time. This phenomenon is why baseball batters waiting their turn to bat warm up with a weight added to their bat. Obviously, the extra mass makes the bat heavier and harder to swing. The batter's strategy is to remove the weight just before stepping up to the plate so the bat will feel lighter and, presumably, can be swung faster.

To a small degree, the weighted bat strategy works. Research shows that batters perceive their bat speed to be faster after having swung a weighted bat rather than a regular bat or a lighter bat. However, the problem is that the perception is an illusion; the feeling of a faster bat swing is a misperception. In fact, research has found that bat swings are actually slower after swinging a weighted bat compared to regular or lighter bats (Southard & Groomer, 2003).

Are these illusions of performance necessarily a bad thing? Perhaps not. In fact, their true effect may be just the opposite. The golfer who believes she can coax the ball to move back into the fairway may feel as though she has greater control than she actually has. The batter who goes to the plate thinking he has a faster swing after warming up with a weighted bat might gain the mental edge needed for facing a tough pitcher. Maybe these illusions increase the person's confidence. Another illusion seems to support that contention.

Baseball players sometimes report that when they are on a hot streak, they perceive pitched balls as larger than normal and, hence, easier to hit (see "The Hot Hand" in chapter 4 for more on streaks of performance). Golfers who are riding the effects of a "hot putter" often report that the hole looks larger than normal. Are these anecdotes merely a part of sport lore, or is there some truth to these perceptions? Jessica Witt and her colleagues investigated these questions and found some evidence to support the anecdotes. In one study, Witt and her colleagues asked softball players to pick out the correct size of the softball from a random grouping of ball sizes arranged on a sheet of paper. Her results revealed a positive correlation between recent batting success and the perceived size of the softball—the more successful the recent performance was, the larger the ball appeared to be. These findings were further explored with a group of golfers to see whether or not recent success correlated with the perceived size of the golf hole. Using similar research methods as before, Witt found once again that success was related to perceptions of size, this time in the form of a negative correlation: people who had attained lower scores (fewer strokes) tended to choose larger holes.

Unfortunately, it is not possible to know the answer to the chicken-versus-egg question from these studies. Is success caused by perceiving the ball or hole to be bigger, or is the inflated perception of size caused by recent success? It seems clear from all of the studies mentioned, however, that perceptual illusions, regardless of their origin, play a real and frequent role in sport performance, in terms of either actual performance outcome or the feeling of anticipated outcome.

SELF-DIRECTED LEARNING ACTIVITIES

1. Define *perceptual illusion* in your own words.
2. The behavior of the craps players has also been called superstitious, because there is no evidence that the behavior has any effect on the outcome. Describe two other types of superstitious behaviors that are typically observed in sport performance.
3. Suggest a hypothesis that would explain why a regular bat feels lighter after warming up with a heavier bat.
4. In his qualitative analysis of cab drivers, Henslin observed that craps players appeared to throw the dice harder or softer depending on the points they were trying to achieve. Describe a research methodology you could use to test Henslin's observations under controlled conditions.

NOTES

- Here is a wonderful video of an illusion of control. In the video (an advertisement for the Qantas Wallabies rugby team), the Australian rugby player attempts a penalty kick, which appears to be headed wide, to the left of the uprights. The player, fans, and people watching on TV all try to coax the ball to curve to go through the uprights by leaning to the right. (Thanks to Clare MacMahon for bringing this video to my attention.)

  www.tinyurl.com/illusioncontrol

- Games of chance include lotteries, dice, and some card games in which the outcome of the game is entirely based on chance; the player has no influence over the odds of winning. Of course, the outcome of rolled dice can be other than chance if the dice are loaded.

- A faster bat swing gives the hitter more time to pick up information about the flight of the ball, making spatial and temporal predictions more accurate (see "Preventing Penalties and Batting Baseballs").

- Most of Jessica Witt's very interesting research papers are listed here:

  www1.psych.purdue.edu/~jkwitt/

SUGGESTED READINGS

Henslin, J.M. (1967). Craps and magic. *American Journal of Sociology, 73,* 316-330.

Langer, E.J. (1975). The illusion of control. *Journal of Personality and Social Psychology, 32,* 311-328.

Southard, D., & Groomer, L. (2003). Warm-up with baseball bats of varying moments of inertia: Effect on bat velocity and swing pattern. *Research Quarterly for Exercise and Sport, 74,* 270-276.

Witt, J.K., Linkenauger, S.A., Bakdash, J.Z., & Proffitt, D.R. (2008). Putting to a bigger hole: Golf performance relates to perceived size. *Psychonomic Bulletin and Review, 15,* 581-585.

Witt, J.K., & Proffitt, D.R. (2005). See the ball, hit the ball: Apparent ball size is correlated with batting average. *Psychological Science, 16,* 937-938.

CHAPTER SIX

ATTENTION

Attention is one of those concepts that has many different connotations, including one discussed in a previous story on inattention blindness ("Turn Right at the Next Gorilla" in chapter 2). The stories in this chapter describe a few more of these attention concepts. Focus of attention underlies the little trick played in "The Toad and the Centipede" fable, which illustrates the disastrous results that can occur when we shift the object to which we direct conscious thought during an action. Attention can also be focused prior to action; this appears to be one of the benefits of applying a consistent preshot routine, as discussed in "The Preshot Routine." One of my pet peeves is the driver who speeds up and slows down during a cell phone conversation, which is explained well by considering attention as limited, like the amount of space available for the ingredients in a gumbo. The attentional limitation described in "Fakes" occurs when two responses are required in a very brief period of time.

THE TOAD AND THE CENTIPEDE

Is an internal or external attentional focus better for improving performance?

The fable goes something like this:

A centipede was happy, quite!
Until a toad, in fun
Said, "Pray, which leg moves after which?"
This raised her doubts to such a pitch
She fell exhausted in the ditch
Not knowing how to run.

Athletes have used the toad's ploy for years. If you are losing your tennis match, try asking your opponent if she is doing something different today, such as coming over the top of the ball to put extra spin on the backhand, or ask your golfing partner whether that right elbow position at the top of the golf swing is something he has been practicing recently. The goal of such a comment is to direct the performer to think about the movement itself, which is not normally a part of movement control, especially in more skilled athletes. Research suggests that athletes who use this ploy might be on to something.

Researchers have speculated about the role of attentional focus in movement control for well over a century, and yet, the concept remains elusive. One reason for this elusiveness is that the concept of attention itself has so many connotations. For example, we can think of attention as something that we *divide*, as when performing two or more actions at the same time. Driving a car while talking on a cell phone is a classic example of dividing your attention between two activities that have different purposes (arriving at a destination versus communicating), sensory modalities (watching traffic versus listening to what someone is saying), and movement systems (using your hands and feet to control the car versus holding a phone and speaking) (for more on this topic, see "Gumbo"). Patting your head while rubbing your belly also requires divided attention. However, this particular activity raises additional motor control concerns because the actions themselves are different. Patting your head and patting your belly, for example, is easy to do even though it involves similar divisions of attention (see "Party Tricks" in chapter 7 for more discussion on this).

A closely related attentional issue concerns selecting to attend to something. For example, if you use a grocery list to shop, then you probably walk up and down the aisles in the store, looking at the shelves with the purpose of finding particular items. The grocery list makes your search very purposeful and specific. Some researchers use the concept of a spotlight as a metaphor for selective attention: we scan the shelves with a rather wide spotlight when we get into the canned goods section, then narrow in when we see the grouping of canned tomatoes, then fine-tune our spotlight even more on the diced tomatoes section as we hone in on the object of our search. The spotlight serves the purpose of both focusing on the object of the search and filtering out the objects that either are neutral to our search (the canned beans) or conflict with the narrow limits of the search (e.g., canned whole tomatoes).

In contrast, think about how you search for groceries if you have forgotten to bring your grocery list. Instead of a very purposefully directed search, you tend to cruise up and down the aisles looking at the shelves for clues about what might have been on that list. In this case, the spotlight has been broadened to include a wider range of potential objects that might meet your search criteria until one object successfully contacts an item in memory, resulting in a narrowing of the spotlight.

Research in motor skills addresses similar issues, although the motor control spotlight often concerns whether attention is focused on the movement itself or the anticipated consequence of the movement. For example, in tennis you might think about how far back to take the racket on the backswing, or how to roll the forearm to impart a downward spin on a forehand shot. Some have labeled this an internal focus of attention because you are directing your mental spotlight inward on how to perform the movement. The attention is internal because the focus is on some combination of the specific motor commands that will result in movement, the sensations that are predicted to result from movement, or the sensations that actually result from the movement. In contrast, instead of focusing on the motor commands and sensations of the movement, you might think about what your intentions are with respect to the environmental impact of your action, such as where you want the ball to go. Researchers refer to this as an external focus of attention because the mental spotlight is moved outside of the body, to an object, destination, impact, or effect that the action will have on the environment.

So what is the relative effectiveness of an internal versus an external focus of attention? The research suggests that their effectiveness depends on the performer's skill level. An internal focus of attention is better suited for beginners, whereas an external focus is more appropriate for experienced performers. The development of motor skill is conceptualized as a process that goes through several stages. Movement control in the earliest stage of learning is highly verbal and proceduralized. For example, when first learning to play the Wii Sport bowling game, I needed to keeping reminding myself to use my index finger to press the B button, on the underside of the remote, at the point of ball release. Fortunately, this verbal, step-by-step type of movement control does not last very long, and we move on to the next stage of learning relatively quickly, depending on the complexity of the task.

Later in learning, movements that had at one time been verbally prompted now seem to be under another level of control, one that no longer requires conscious attention. Some researchers use the term *automaticity* to refer to this level of control. After hours of playing Wii Sport bowling, I no longer had to consciously remind myself to press the B button to release the ball, where the button is located, or what finger to use to press the button. Instead, all of these actions became subservient to higher-order actions or intentions. In games that are more complex than this video example, or in many activities of daily living, these higher-order intentions might include specific strategies or goal-related actions. For example, we don't think about the movements involved in walking when crossing a busy street, but focus instead on the flow of pedestrian traffic and curbs to step over to ensure a safe passage.

Accordingly, some researchers have predicted that having experts focus on the mechanics of their actions would be detrimental to performance because they are naturally performing in an externally focused manner. This was the thinking of Sian Beilock and her colleagues when they asked a group of highly skilled golfers and a group of novice golfers to make putts under various experimental conditions. In one experiment, Beilock and her colleagues asked golfers to either take their time and try to be as accurate as possible with the putt or execute the putt as soon as possible after the setup. The effects of these instructions were entirely dependent on the skill level of the golfer. For novice golfers, the accuracy instruction resulted in better putting than did the speed instruction. However, the reverse was true for the experts: spending *less* time thinking about the putt produced better performance than spending more time.

A second experiment by the Beilock research group confirmed and extended these findings. In this experiment the groups of golfers putted either while thinking about the putt or being distracted by a secondary task (monitoring an auditory tone). As in the previous study, the novices benefited most when thinking about the putt. The opposite was true for the experts: being distracted from thinking about the putt produced their best performances.

These findings, along with other studies published from Rob Gray's lab and our own lab, support the idea that focus of attention effects are specific to the skill level of the performer. The beginner needs to focus on the movement itself because of both the uncertainty of what needs to be done and how closely the actions of the body will respond to the person's intentions. More highly skilled performers no longer have such uncertainty; they have a good idea of what needs to be done and how to do it. Focusing on the intended consequences of the action leaves the details of movement control to a level that is very well learned and no longer requires conscious monitoring.

The task of coordinating all those pairs of legs would seem impossible if the centipede were thinking about which leg moved with which. Like the clever athlete who asks her opponent how she is producing such good shots today, the toad is trying to get the centipede to shift her thinking from an external to an internal attentional focus. The toad appeared to take great delight in messing with the centipede's mind.

SELF-DIRECTED LEARNING ACTIVITIES

1. Define *attentional focus* in your own words.
2. What do the terms *top-down processing* and *bottom-up processing* refer to when describing visual attention theory, and how do they relate specifically to the example of shopping in the story?
3. Suggest reasons why an internal focus of attention might disrupt the performance of a skilled musician.
4. Describe another sport task or activity of daily living that could be performed with either an internal or an external focus of attention. Devise a research methodology to investigate the effects of these focus-of-attention conditions on performance.

NOTES

• The author of the fable is unknown.

SUGGESTED READINGS

Beilock, S.L. (2010). *Choke: What the secrets of the brain reveal about getting it right when you have to.* New York: Free Press.

Beilock, S.L., & Gonso, S. (2008). Putting in the mind vs. putting on the green: Expertise, performance time, and the linking of imagery and action. *The Quarterly Journal of Experimental Psychology: Human Experimental Psychology, 61,* 920-932.

Castaneda, B., & Gray, R. (2007). Effects of focus of attention on baseball batting performance in players of differing skill levels. *Journal of Sport & Exercise Psychology, 29,* 60-77.

Perkins-Ceccato, N., Passmore, S.R., & Lee, T.D. (2003). Effects of focus of attention depend on golfers' skill. *Journal of Sports Sciences, 21,* 593-600.

Schmidt, R.A., & Lee, T.D. (2011). Attention and performance. In *Motor control and learning: A behavioral emphasis* (5th ed., pp. 97-132) Champaign, IL: Human Kinetics.

Wulf, G. (2007). *Attention and motor skill learning.* Champaign, IL: Human Kinetics.

THE PRESHOT ROUTINE

Why does a consistent mental preparation ritual benefit performance?

Watch any professional athlete perform an action in which the initiation of movement is under his or her control (a self-paced task), such as taking a free throw in basketball, hitting a golf ball, or stroking a cue ball in billiards. What you will see with most athletes is an activity that is repeated the same way, time and again, just prior to each action, called the preshot (or preperformance) routine. Golfers, in particular, have unique preshot routines. In his practice swing, Mike Weir takes the club back about halfway and then returns it to a position behind the ball, just before he takes his full swing. At the moment Jim Furyk looks to be about to take a putting stroke, he backs away to assess the line. Basketball players perform a similar activity at the free throw line. They may bounce the ball a certain number of times or roll it around in their hands, but again, they have their own particular way of preparing. These athletes may not make the putt or sink the free throw every time, but they always start with the same preshot routine, and they try to do it the same way every time.

This type of behavior leads to two questions that seem rather obvious: do preshot routines work, and if so, why? The first question has been addressed in a number of ways. Sport psychologists contend that a consistent preshot routine is one of the most important parts of becoming an elite golfer, and golfers often contend that their performance improved only after they had established a consistent preshot routine.

But how valid and reliable are these anecdotes? Experimental evidence using expert performers is difficult to gather because elite athletes (such as PGA touring professionals) are generally unwilling to depart from their preshot routines, even for a brief experiment. Using an alternative research strategy to investigate the effects of a preshot routine, researchers compared groups of subjects who had never played golf before with groups who played frequently but were not highly skilled. Two groups of golfers from each skill level completed a three-week training program in which they practiced a wedge shot from varying distances either with or without an accompanying preshot routine. Their results from two posttraining tests are illustrated in figure 6.1, along with those of a control group that did not participate in the training program. Clearly, both the golfers and nongolfers benefited from the three weeks of training, because they performed better on the posttests than the control groups did. More important, though, both the golfers and

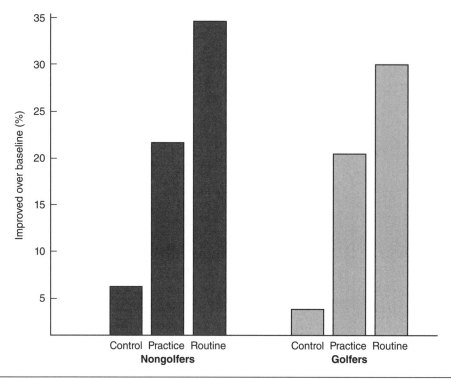

Figure 6.1   Effects of a preshot routine on performance improvement.
Graph prepared from data presented in McCann, Lavallee, and Lavallee (2001).

nongolfers obtained an advantage from using a consistent preshot routine along with their physical practice trials.

The specific reasons a preshot routine would benefit performance could be explained by a variety of theories. One is that a consistent routine instills confidence, and the positive outlook on an upcoming action enhances performance. An alternative suggestion is that the preshot routine helps the athlete to focus attention on the external factors most important to successful performance, such as specific visual cues in the environment. As discussed previously (see "The Toad and the Centipede"), an appropriate focus of attention has a critical impact on movement control.

Still another view relates the preshot routine to a curious finding in the motor control literature called warm-up decrement (see also "Shooting Two From the Line" in chapter 11). This refers to the drop in performance that occurs when a rest or delay period precedes the initiation of movement. The delay period could be relatively short (e.g., minutes), such as the delay between putting on two consecutive golf holes, or much longer, such as between situations in which a sand bunker shot is required (which might be several rounds of golf apart). Some believe that losing a specific mind-set for performing the task in a particular manner is responsible for the warm-up decrement. An appropriate preshot routine might provide an effective means to overcome this lost mind-set. In so doing, the preshot routine counteracts the negative impact of warm-up decrement.

If distracted at the last moment, Annika Sorenstam (one of the best golfers in the history of the game) was known to stop her preshot routine, back away from the ball, put her club back in the bag, put the head cover back on the club, and then start the preshot routine all over again (Nilsson, Marriott, & Sirak, 2005). Although the research is not entirely clear about why the preshot routine is important in motor skill performance, it is almost certain that a consistent preshot routine has a beneficial impact on performance.

SELF-DIRECTED LEARNING ACTIVITIES

1. Define the term *preshot* (or *preperformance*) *routine* in your own words.
2. Describe what a successful preshot routine might entail.
3. Describe a specific pre–free throw routine of any NBA basketball player. Why do you believe he uses this particular routine?
4. Develop an experimental methodology for assessing the effects of a preshot routine. Assume that you could persuade a professional athlete to take part in your experiment.

NOTES

- The golf manufacturer Titleist has a gallery of videos showing the preshot routines of some professional golfers:

  www.tinyurl.com/preshotroutines

- The term *warm-up*, as used in the term *warm-up decrement*, does not imply warming up in the sense of being physically ready for action. Rather, it refers to getting into the proper psychological frame of reference. Although not very recent, the following reference remains one of the best reviews of the research on this topic:

  Adams, J.A. (1961). The second facet of forgetting: A review of warm-up decrement. *Psychological Bulletin, 58,* 257-273.

SUGGESTED READINGS

Hellström, J. (2009). Psychological hallmarks of skilled golfers. *Sports Medicine, 39,* 845-855.

McCann, P., Lavallee, D., & Lavallee, R.M. (2001). The effect of pre-shot routines on golf wedge shot performance. *European Journal of Sport Science, 1*(5), 1-10.

Nilsson, P., Marriott, L., & Sirak, R. (2005). *Every shot must have a purpose.* New York: Gotham Books.

What are the limits
of attentional capacity?

You can predict it with almost 100 percent certainty. The driver in front of you speeds up, then slows down, speeds up, then slows down again. Occasionally, the car veers over one of the lines that define the lane, only to get jerked back abruptly into place. Finally, you have had enough and decide to pass. As you go past the car, you shoot a quick look at the driver. Is the driver drunk? Nope, worse. He is talking on a cell phone.

Is driving while talking on a cell phone really similar to drunk driving? Some researchers think so. They believe that a driver's capability to safely operate a motor vehicle is severely impaired while talking on a cell phone, just as it is when intoxicated on alcohol. Others suggest that it is only a problem if the driver is using a handheld cell phone—that a hands-free phone eliminates the problem. These and other issues have been the objects of legal discussion worldwide since cell phones became an indispensable part of our culture, and have resulted in a wide assortment of laws, debates, and experimental studies.

The problem concerns the issue of attention, which, as I have discussed in the other stories in this chapter, is a rather diverse and complex topic. The issue of cell phone use while driving is about divided attention. Specifically, the question is this: How much, or in how many ways, can we divide our attention before performance starts to suffer?

The answer is not a simple one. And in fact, it is not just a matter of how many ways attention can be divided. For example, I can tap my right index finger rhythmically by itself, together with the index finger of my left hand, or together with my left hand and both feet; dividing attention among all four effectors produces a rhythmic performance that is as good as the rhythmic tapping of one finger by itself. In fact, research suggests that rhythmic timing performance actually improves when multiple effectors are tapping together (Helmuth & Ivry, 1996). When all four of the parts converge to achieve a common goal, then the attention devoted to each one is no greater than the attention paid to the collective whole.

The problem of divided attention occurs when each of the parts has an action goal that is separate and unique from that of the others. For example, instead of tapping both hands, try rubbing your head and patting your tummy at the same time (see "Party Tricks" in chapter 7). This task is difficult because the two parts have no common action goal. Instead, each limb has its own unique action, with differing movement commands and sensory feedback that must be monitored during performance to achieve its distinct goal. Each part requires individualized attention to achieve accurate performance.

When researchers talk about the division of attention, they often refer to the concept of capacity—the fact that we have an absolute limit to the amount of attention we can devote to the processes involved in thinking and doing. Presumably, everyone has an absolute limit, or amount, of capacity to allocate flexibly to the performance of certain tasks. An analogy might work well here to illustrate these points.

Let's say that a large pot can hold up to 10 liters of gumbo. If the recipe calls for a combined 6 liters of water and rice, then only 4 liters of space remain for the other ingredients. I have a total volume of 6 liters of chicken, sausage, shrimp, and vegetables to add to the pot. I can fit more of these ingredients in the pot if I reduce the amount of water and rice. But, doing so changes the nature and essence of the recipe. Alternatively, I could maintain the amount of rice and water (6 liters) and add all of my other ingredients too (6 liters). If I do that, however, then some of the water and rice is going to spill onto the stove, leaving a mess to clean up.

By analogy, the attention needed for safely driving a car will occupy a large portion of my available capacity. I can add other things to the mix, such as listening to the radio, carrying on a conversation with someone else in the car, drinking a cup of coffee, thinking about work to be done at the office, and so on. And the degree to which these can be safely added to the driving task will depend on the attentional capacity required by each. The potential for problems begins once the total of the attention required by all of the tasks exceeds the limited amount of attentional capacity. To reduce the potential for problems, I must reduce the total attention demanded by the tasks being performed so that they do not exceed my available capacity. In other words, everything must fit in the gumbo pot. This could involve eliminating one or more of the extra tasks or reducing the attention devoted to each. I could also reduce the attention devoted to driving. However, like the gumbo analogy, reducing the main ingredients has the potential to ruin the recipe and produce disastrous results.

Drivers who talk on their cell phones often exceed their available attentional capacity. Their pot overflows. Others who share the road hope that the driver prevents this overflow by reducing the amount of attention devoted to the phone conversation. That is, they hope that the driver prevents the attentional gumbo pot from overflowing by maximally attending to the demands of the driving task and reducing the attention paid to the phone conversation. But we all know that this decision is not always followed, and evidence overwhelmingly shows that talking on a cell phone while driving increases the probability of an accident, perhaps by as much as fourfold. All too often the driver responds to the overflow either by reducing the amount of attention devoted to driving (resulting in all kinds of bad driving behaviors) or by simply allowing the pot to overflow, leading to an accident.

The issues and questions about distracted driving are far more complex than this, however. Consider the following questions.

1. *Are the attentional capacity demands for driving the same for all people?* Clearly not. The attention a novice driver needs in order to operate a motor vehicle in traffic is far greater than the attention a highly experienced driver needs. Therefore, in theory, the experienced driver should have more available capacity for a cell phone conversation than does the novice.

2. *Do all conversations require equal capacity?* Again, the answer to this is an obvious no. In your kitchen you can fix a sandwich while talking on the phone up to the point at which something very important in the conversation arises, at which time you stop the sandwich making and devote much more capacity to what the other person is saying.

3. *Do handheld cell phones require more capacity than hands-free units?* Again, the research has yielded a very clear answer: the attention demanded by the conversation is the critical issue, not the demands of holding a phone. Almost every study conducted on this topic showed no difference in the capacity demands of handheld and hands-free phones (despite what lawmakers believe).

4. *Does talking on a cell phone demand more attention than talking to other people in the car, or listening to the radio?* Remember that a cell phone conversation has no fixed amount of demanded capacity, and the same is true for conversations with people in a car, radio programs, e-mail, text messages, and attending to GPS maps. Depending on the nature of the task, all have the capability to demand a dangerous amount of attention while driving. But again, research is very clear on this issue: carrying on a conversation with a passenger in the car demands less attention than does a cell phone conversation.

So, is driving while talking on a cell phone equivalent to driving while intoxicated? Actually, the question is a not an appropriate one. The elevated attention demands of the cell phone call can be changed simply by making a conscious decision to pay more attention to driving or hanging up; the decrement due to intoxication cannot be dismissed by the will of the driver. On the other hand, the roads would be much safer without either type of driver.

SELF-DIRECTED LEARNING ACTIVITIES

1. Define *attentional capacity* in your own words.
2. I have used the gumbo pot as an analogy to explain attentional capacity and demands. Create a different analogy to explain these concepts.
3. Develop an experimental methodology to examine the attentional capacity of driving when combined with any two of the following

factors: (a) using a hands-free versus handheld cell phones, (b) having a conversation with a passenger, (c) reading a GPS display, (d) listening to the radio, and (e) text messaging.

4. Compose a letter to your legislative representative stating your position on the legality of cell phone use while driving.

NOTES

- Why do people insist on using cheesy ring tones such as "Edelweiss"?
- An epidemiological study done in Toronto found that drivers were four times more likely to be involved in an accident when talking on a cell phone:

  Redelmeier, D.A., & Tibshirani, R.J. (1997). Association between cellular-telephone calls and motor vehicle collisions. *The New England Journal of Medicine, 336,* 453-458.

- This research suggests that conversations with passengers are both less attention demanding than cell phone conversations and different, often because the traffic becomes a topic of conversation:

  Drews, F.A., Pasupathi, M., & Strayer, D.L. (2008). Passenger and cell phone conversations in simulated driving. *Journal of Experimental Psychology: Applied, 14,* 392–400.

SUGGESTED READINGS

Helmuth, L.L., & Ivry, R.B. (1996). When two hands are better than one: Reduced timing variability during bimanual movement. *Journal of Experimental Psychology: Human Perception and Performance, 22,* 278-293.

McCartt, A.T., Hellinga, L.A., & Bratiman, K.A. (2006). Cell phones and driving: Review of research. *Traffic Injury Prevention, 7,* 89-106.

Schmidt, R.A., & Lee, T.D. (2011). Attention and performance. In *Motor control and learning: A behavioral emphasis* (5th ed., pp. 97-132) Champaign, IL: Human Kinetics.

FAKES

What role does the psychological refractory period play in sport?

Highlight videos on sport newscasts often feature dynamic plays of the day. Some of the most spectacular of these are the fakes: Steve Nash drives toward the net, looks one way, and makes a no-look pass the other way; or Sidney Crosby fakes a shot to the upper left corner of the goal and then deftly moves the puck to the backhand to slide it past the goalie and into the right corner of the net. What makes the fake so fascinating is the response of the other person: he reacts to the initial move and then seems to be frozen in time, unable to respond to the change in plans when the final move is made.

Why do fakes work, and when don't they work? Many people believe that to make a fake work, the athlete has to sell it well. That is, the initial action has to be believable enough that the defender will react to it, thinking that this will be the action that needs to be defended. However, what comes after the initial move, and when it comes, determines how well the fake works.

One key element in making the fake work is the time between the two actions of the offensive player. Researchers have studied a similar type of experimental situation for many years. Essentially, a fake that works is one in which the defensive player is caught in a kind of cognitive limbo, what researchers refer to as the psychological refractory period. In biology, a refractory period refers to the latency of time following the excitation of a membrane during which it cannot be excited again. The membrane must return to its resting state before a stimulus can once again excite it. The term *psychological refractory period* was meant to convey a similar idea, although the processes involved appear to be more complex.

Research on the psychological refractory period has typically used a particular experimental situation, which I have illustrated in figure 6.2 *a* and *b*, using Steve Nash as an example. The bottom left gray bar in figure 6.2*b* illustrates the time the defender takes to react to the fake look to the right, and the much longer gray bar on the bottom right side of the figure illustrates the reaction to the real pass. The illustration simply shows that the reaction time to the real shot is much slower.

Note, however, that the comparison of the reaction time to the faked pass to the reaction time to the real pass is *not* the appropriate one to make. Rather, the reaction time to the real pass that either follows a fake (figure 6.2*b*) or does not follow a fake (figure 6.2*a*) is the appropriate comparison.

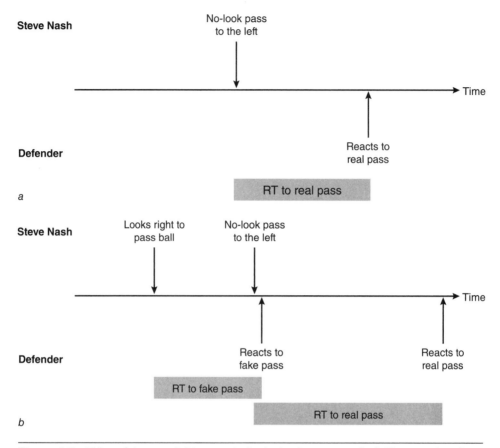

Figure 6.2 When fakes work (the psychological refractory period). The reaction time to a pass without a fake is shown in (*a*). The reaction time to a pass following a fake (*b*) is much longer.

In other words, how is the defender's reaction time to the real pass affected by whether it is preceded by the fake to the right or not preceded by the fake? The most important information in figure 6.2 *a* and *b* is the lengths of the gray bars illustrating the reaction time of the defender to the fake shot and the real shot.

The psychological refractory period refers to the (nonspecific) effect of having to respond to a second stimulus before the response to a first stimulus has been completed. In figure 6.2*a*, the reaction time to the real pass was relatively fast because there was no preceding stimulus, thus, no refractory period from which the respondent needed to recover before another reaction could be initiated. However, in figure 6.2*b*, the reaction time was delayed because the defender was trying to recover from processing and responding to the fake. The psychological refractory period refers to that period of time when a reaction to the second move must be delayed until the processing system is ready to go again.

Now, let's deal with the second issue: when do fakes *not* work? Again, research concerning the psychological refractory period provides some good ideas. Essentially, the reaction time to the real pass would be expected to be relatively short if the second move occurred either too soon or too long after the fake. Waiting too long after the fake (see figure 6.3*b*) gives the defender enough time to complete the refractory period, and therefore, the defender should be completely recovered and ready to respond quickly to the real pass.

The situation in figure 6.3*a* represents a case where Steve Nash does not wait long enough after the initial move (the fake look to the right) before starting the real pass to the left. Not waiting long enough after the fake represents a more interesting challenge to explain, and the research is not entirely clear about why this occurs. Perhaps the defender can cancel or inhibit the reaction to the fake before it begins, or perhaps the real shot comes before the defender even begins the reaction, and so he is fully prepared to respond to the real shot. Or maybe time is just an important part of selling the fake. In all, a fake not only is a visually interesting highlight to watch on TV but is fascinating and challenging to study as well.

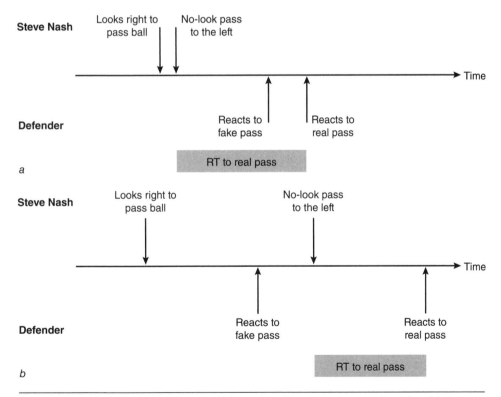

Figure 6.3 When fakes do not work. Reaction time to a pass made either (*a*) too soon after a fake or (*b*) too long after a fake will not likely be slowed by a psychological refractory period.

SELF-DIRECTED LEARNING ACTIVITIES

1. Define *psychological refractory period* in your own words.
2. Name two other factors, other than the time between the fake and real stimulus, that would influence the length of the reaction time to the real stimulus.
3. Describe how a psychological refractory period after a fake would work in a sport other than hockey or basketball.
4. Develop a methodology that would allow you to measure the duration of a psychological refractory period in the sport identified in question 3.

NOTES

- Only the defender's reaction time is being discussed here. In fact, the situation is complicated by the fact that the defender has moved to block the (faked) shot, and now is in both a psychological refractory period and at a biomechanical disadvantage to stop the real shot.

SUGGESTED READINGS

Klein, R.M. (2000). Inhibition of return. *Trends in Cognitive Sciences, 4,* 138-147.

Lien, M.C., & Proctor, R.W. (2002). Stimulus-response compatibility and psychological refractory period effects: Implications for response selection. *Psychonomic Bulletin & Review, 9,* 212-238.

Schmidt, R.A., & Lee, T.D. (2011). Attention and performance. In *Motor control and learning: A behavioral emphasis* (5th ed., pp. 97-132) Champaign, IL: Human Kinetics.

MOTOR CONTROL

As we have seen, action is a complex relationship that brings together many features of cognition that include attention, perception, decision making, and memory. But the study of motor control is an important area of research in and of itself. This chapter presents some stories that highlight various theoretical positions about how we control our ongoing actions. In "Websites and Silly Walks," we see that flexibility and redundancy help us achieve specific goals without having to repeat anything exactly the same way time and again. Leave it to a Canadian, in "The Curling Draw," to explain closed-loop control as an analogy to playing a game on ice. The skill of using visual information to fill in the times when we are not looking at something is the basis for "Cool Papa Bell," which is about a baseball player who always did things quickly. Anticipating and predicting what will happen, and then controlling our movements in a preemptive manner, are the theme of both "Moving Sidewalks and Beer Glasses" and "The Tickle." The study of motor programs (which is discussed in "Antilock Brakes" in chapter 5) is discussed further in two stories: "The Point of No Return" and "Forensic Motor Control." Here we find out that the motor program concept has varying identities, each with compelling research issues. The topic of coordinating independently moving parts concludes this chapter in the stories "Party Tricks" and "Disappearing Act." Don't forget to pack your finger pistols when reading these stories.

How do redundancies help us solve motor problems?

One of the features of an effective web page is redundancy: websites often have two or more routes that you can take to achieve the same result. For example, suppose you wanted to order the CD recently released by your favorite band. On the band's website is a picture of the new CD, and clicking on that image will take you to the order page. Off to the right side is a flashing pop-up advertising the new CD; clicking on it will also take you to the order page. Along the left side is a list of website options, including one that says, "Merchandise." Clicking it will take you to a page that lists the CDs available for purchase, including the new one. The redundancy in the website provides multiple ways to achieve the same result: ordering the CD.

Our motor control system is built like an effective website. Consider the goal of removing a screw cap from a bottle of water, for example. You can hold the bottle in your left hand and turn the cap with your right, or hold the cap and turn the bottle. You can hold the bottle in your right hand and turn the cap with your left, or the other way around. You can turn the cap using the palm of your hand; you can use your thumb and index finger; in fact, you can grasp it between any two fingers. You can hold the bottle close to your chest or with outstretched arms. You can open the bottle while sitting down, standing up, walking, or running a marathon. You can open it quickly or slowly. In fact, you can open the bottle in an infinite number of ways—and these are just the observable differences! We can open a thousand bottles using what looks to be the same method, and still the way the neuromuscular details are organized by the central nervous system will differ every time. And yet, through all of these myriad ways, we never fail to find a solution to the problem of opening the bottle of water.

Locomotion provides us with another example of redundancy. Humans typically use one of two gaits to get from point A to point B—walking or running. However, we can also hop or skip if we so choose. But these are just four of the infinite number of ways we can locomote. One of the most memorable sketches of the English comedy series *Monty Python's Flying Circus* was called the "Ministry of Silly Walks." It featured John Cleese and the cast members performing hilarious yet motorically quite inventive adaptations to the ways we normally walk. These were all achieved because of the redundancies in our central nervous system, the ability to flexibly solve the problem of locomoting from point A to point B.

People with movement constraints provide good examples of how redundancies are used to solve motor problems. Those who are born without upper limbs develop an amazing ability to use their legs and feet to solve the problems that most people solve using their arms and hands. Those without the use of an opposable thumb devise strategies, learn capabilities, and use substitutions to provide the opposition that many take for granted in such activities as grasping. And we have probably all seen artists who paint masterful works by holding paintbrushes in their mouths. These are just a few examples of how the central nervous system can be reorganized to solve motor problems.

The environment can also limit our ability to exploit our motor system's redundancies. Taking the cap off the water bottle, for example, requires a counterclockwise turn of the cap. The environment (human made, in this instance) has put some constraints on what actions will be successful in solving the problem. Extremely tight-fitting pants would have constrained some of John Cleese's silly walks. In fact, the very nature of some situations can restrict our movements. The mouse pad I am using right now has a workspace of 6 by 8 1/2 inches (15 by 21.6 cm). The size of the mouse pad workspace constrains the way I navigate around the desktop on my computer. For example, I could use my left hand to navigate the mouse, but doing so would be awkward, inefficient, and prone to errors. Nevertheless, I have an immense number of possible solutions available to me for using my right arm and hand to solve the navigation issues.

Constraints on the flexibility of our motor solutions can also be intentional or learned. As children, we are taught to hold our pens and pencils in our hands in a certain way. There are endless numbers of ways to hold our writing instruments, but many of us have either not learned these options or were actively discouraged from using them in childhood. The golf swing has about as many solutions as there are golfers in the world. And yet, most instructors try to encourage their students to adapt their swings to match a particular model. Constraints on motor solutions are imposed on us so that our movements conform to a common solution.

The point here is that humans have vast flexibility in the way they solve motor problems. When constraints are few, the adaptability of the system seems endless. When constraints are many, we tend to solve the problems in more stereotypical ways. Regardless, we possess a central nervous system that uses many redundancies and modes of control to find and optimize solutions. The following stories describe some of these modes of control.

SELF-DIRECTED LEARNING ACTIVITIES

1. Define *movement redundancy* in your own words.
2. Describe a system other than a website in which a solution can be achieved in two or more ways.

3. Provide a different example of how the motor system solves problems in redundant ways.

4. Describe three environmental constraints that would influence the creation of a new silly walk.

Notes

- Some YouTube videos of Monty Python's routine:
    www.tinyurl.com/montypython1
    www.tinyurl.com/montypython2
- Create your own silly walk!
    www.sillywalksgenerator.com

Suggested Readings

Davids, K., Button, C., & Bennett, S. (2008). *Dynamics of skill acquisition: A constraints-led approach.* Champaign, IL: Human Kinetics.

Turvey, M.T. (1990). Coordination. *American Psychologist, 45,* 938-953.

What sport skills use open- and closed-loop systems of motor control?

Curling is a sport played on ice. It is similar in concept to games such as shuffleboard, bocce, horseshoes, and darts, in which the goal is to propel an object toward a target. However, what makes curling unique is that, unlike these other sports and games, players have some control over the object once they have released it. In shuffleboard, the person who pushed the disk along the floor or table has no control over the location of the its final resting spot after the disk is on its way. The same is true for bocce, horseshoes, darts, and most other target games. But, this is not so in curling.

The basic goal in curling is to slide round granite rocks along a sheet of ice toward a bull's-eye. Two teams of four players alternate sliding each of their rocks. The goal is to have as many of your rocks as close as possible to the center of the concentric rings painted on the ice. Sometimes the appropriate strategy is a take-out, in which you run one of your rocks into your opponent's rock(s); at other times the appropriate strategy is to play a draw, in which you try to propel the rock with just the right amount of force to have it stop at an exact spot on the ice. Figure 7.1 illustrates a curling draw.

The ice sheet in curling is about 50 yards (45 m) long, and a rock weighs about 44 pounds (20 kg). Therefore, a considerable amount of force is required to slide the rock the full length of the sheet. One member of the team starts by pushing off from a fixed start point and sliding along the ice while holding on to a handle attached to the rock. The curler must let go of the handle at some point before crossing a line that is painted on the ice. At that point, the curler is about 30 yards (28 m) to the middle of the rings. We know from research concerning Fitts' law (see "The Calculator" in chapter 3) and Schmidt's law (see "The Gimme Putt" in chapter 3) that accuracy and consistency in aiming tasks degrade quickly as the distance to the target increases, or as the force applied to an object increases. In the case of curling, a heavy object is being propelled a long distance, over a duration of 10 to 20 seconds, to a very small spot on the ice—a very challenging task indeed!

To make the draw shot a little more precise, the rules of curling allow any or all of the members of the team to use broomlike objects to rub the ice just ahead of the curling rock. Rubbing with the brooms causes the ice to melt temporarily, reducing the friction between the ice and the rock and thereby

Figure 7.1 A curling draw.
Xinhua/Zuma Press/Icon SMI

causing the rock to lose speed at a reduced rate and to slide straighter than it would otherwise. Many players use this strategy, sometimes starting and stopping the brushing as appropriate, to ensure that the rock achieves its final targeted resting point.

In shuffleboard, archery, darts, and most other targeting games, players have no control over the object once they have released it. The control of the flight of the object in these games involves what is called an open-loop process: the performer's influence over the final position of the object is complete once the performer is no longer in contact with the object. The take-out shot in curling is an open-loop process too, because the rock is slid with considerable speed (faster than the sweepers can keep up) and force (leaving little opportunity for melted ice to have an effect on the path of the rock). In contrast, the control of the speed and path of a draw shot is accomplished by what is called a closed-loop process. The process is illustrated in figure 7.2.

Essentially, figure 7.2 represents a closed-loop process in which there is a continuous assessment of the status of the rock with respect to its intended final position on the ice. If the rock is moving too fast, nothing can be done to slow it down. The curling team has to hope that the friction between the

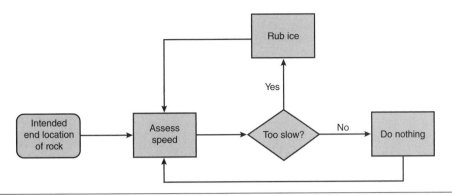

Figure 7.2   The closed-loop process of achieving a final location in a curling draw.

rock and the ice will be sufficient to stop the rock in time. However, the team must continue to monitor the status of the rock, because if it slows down too much, players will need to rub the ice to maintain its speed. This is a closed-loop process because the players are continuously assessing the status of the rock and comparing it to its intended goal. It is called a closed-loop process because all lines of communication feed back to a decision maker to maintain equilibrium with respect to the intended goal. Hence, a closed-loop system is one that depends on feedback.

Curling is a nice example of both the open-loop and closed-loop processes and provides an effective illustration of one of the important systems of motor control used by humans. Essentially, given sufficient time, we use information feedback derived from our senses to modify actions after they have been initiated. As the curling rock demonstrates, we need sufficient time to process the feedback to use the information effectively. Therefore, closed-loop motor control processes depend on the total duration of the movement and speed with which we can use sensory feedback. Consequently, researchers have spent considerable effort trying to understand how motor control is influenced when closed-loop processes are available, and the modes of control that are available when closed-loop control is unavailable. In the next story ("Cool Papa Bell"), I describe how one type of information feedback (i.e., vision) is used to regulate movement.

SELF-DIRECTED LEARNING ACTIVITIES

1. In your own words, define and distinguish between an open-loop system and a closed-loop system.

2. Modify the closed-loop flowchart in figure 7.2 to describe how you would use visual feedback to thread a needle.

3. Aside from vision, what other types of sensory feedback are commonly used for the closed-loop control of movement? Give examples of situations in which these forms of feedback would be used.

4. Search the literature to find a study in which researchers determined the minimum amount of time required to use visual feedback to control movement. Describe the specific methodology used.

NOTES

- The dimensions of a curling sheet are shown in this diagram:
  www.mycurling.com/articles/curlingsheet.html
- Although called curling "rocks," they are actually finely made pieces of rounded granite, concave on the bottom and highly polished to slide easily along the ice.
- A few things about the flowchart: decisions are denoted by triangles, actions are denoted by rectangles, feedback and lines of communication are denoted by arrows.
- The senses studied most in human motor control are vision and proprioception, although auditory feedback and tactile feedback are very important sources of information as well.
- This Wikipedia article provides a nice overview of the sport of curling:
  http://en.wikipedia.org/wiki/curling

SUGGESTED READINGS

Bradley, J. (2009). The sports science of curling: A practical review. *Journal of Sports Science and Medicine, 8,* 495-500.

Schmidt, R.A., & Lee, T.D. (2011). Sensory contributions to motor control. In *Motor control and learning: A behavioral emphasis* (5th ed., pp. 135-176) Champaign, IL: Human Kinetics.

When vision is interrupted, how does iconic memory guide motor tasks?

Cool Papa Bell was a star baseball player in the U.S. Negro Leagues for more than 20 years during the early 20th century. He was a superb outfielder and batter and was elected to the Hall of Fame in 1974. What Cool Papa Bell was probably remembered most for, however, was his speed on the base paths. Legend has it that he once scored from first base on a bunted ball and that he could circle the bases faster than any player of his time, black or white. In fact, fellow Hall of Fame member Josh Gibson once said, "Cool Papa Bell was so fast he could get out of bed, turn out the lights across the room and be back in bed under the covers before the lights went out." Although it sounds ridiculous, Gibson may have been right!

It goes without saying that vision is a critical component of most activities of daily living, such as walking along a path, guiding a mouse-controlled cursor to an icon on your computer desktop, or even just pouring a glass of milk. All of these examples require precise aiming—from placing a footstep on the path, acquiring the target with a cursor, or guiding the flow of liquid into a container. Quite simply, actions that require vision for successful completion are doomed to fail if you can't see what you're doing.

But, in the absence of vision, how soon would a visually guided task be doomed to fail? Research suggests that we do not need to continuously watch something to use the visual information accurately. Rather, we possess a very accurate, albeit short-lived, sensory memory that fills in the details when we glance away or when something blocks our line of sight. This sensory memory system appears to be distinct from the memory that we use, say, to look up and retain a phone number while dialing it, or the memory that we use to retrieve the name and image of our first-grade teacher. The visual sensory memory is an iconic representation of an object or the environment in general. Research suggests that our iconic memory can be used as a faithful substitute for a short period of time when vision is obstructed or averted.

Together with his students and colleagues, researcher Digby Elliott studied the processing of visual information in many experimental situations. In some studies, he gathered people in a large gymnasium and asked them to walk to targets located on the floor a short distance away. In other experiments, he asked them to throw objects at these targets. Before beginning an activity, the participants were told to close their eyes so that the target was no longer directly visible. What he found was that people were surprisingly accurate at these tasks in the absence of vision. In fact, there was often no decrement in performance at all when the activity was completed within two seconds of removing vision! Apparently, the visual memory of the target was a sufficient and reliable substitute for direct visual information and could faithfully guide the action.

But, some speculated, perhaps the participants in Elliott's research performed so well without vision simply because the targets were stationary. How would they perform if the task involved a moving object, such as catching a ball? Would they need a continuous supply of visual information to be successful? Once again, Elliott provided a provocative answer to the question. In a further series of experiments, Elliott and his colleagues asked participants to wear special goggles while catching tennis balls projected from a ball machine about 10 yards (9 m) away. These goggles could be programmed to alternate between being clear (providing a full view of the ball) and being clouded (letting in light but eliminating any information about the flight of the ball). Remarkably, Elliott found that catching performance remained excellent when snapshots of vision as short as 20 milliseconds were alternated with periods of no vision as long as 80 milliseconds. Moreover, success was not improved by increasing the length of the visual snapshot. Instead, performance degraded quickly when the periods without vision were increased to 100 milliseconds and longer.

Digby Elliott's research reveals quite nicely that we have a dependable visual representation of our static immediate surroundings that allows us to move about and interact without accidents for relatively long periods of time. Moreover, we do not need continuous vision of our dynamic environment either: updated information that is provided with a frequency as low as 10 times per second (Hz) will still permit us to perform actions safely and efficiently.

Could Cool Papa Bell actually get into bed before the lights went out, as Josh Gibson reported? Well, it all depends on what you consider as the lights going out. For Bell, the vision of his bedroom layout and where he had to go to get back into bed without tripping could have been faithfully represented for plenty of time to allow him to get back safely under the covers. And don't forget, he was very fast.

SELF-DIRECTED LEARNING ACTIVITIES

1. Define *iconic memory* in your own words.
2. How could iconic memory fit in the closed-loop flowchart model for a curling draw described in the previous story?
3. What role do you think iconic memory serves when we blink?
4. Reenact one of Elliott's walking or throwing eyes-closed experiments. Do your findings replicate his results?

NOTES

- The National Baseball Hall of Fame site includes more information on Cool Papa Bell, along with a link to the speech he gave upon induction into the Hall of Fame:

    http://baseballhall.org/hof/bell-cool-papa

- The Wikipedia article on Cool Papa Bell includes several more stories about his legendary speed:

    http://en.wikipedia.org/wiki/cool_papa_bell

- Artificial light, computer monitors, and televisions are just some of the devices that use intermittent periods of light and dark. We perceive these intermittencies as flicker when the cycles occur at less than a critical fusion point, which depends on a large number of environmental and other factors, but which is generally less than 50 Hz.

SUGGESTED READINGS

Elliott, D. (1990). Intermittent visual pickup and goal directed movement: A review. *Human Movement Science, 9,* 531-548.

Elliott, D., & Khan, M.A. (2010). *Vision and goal-directed movement: Neurobehavioral perspectives.* Champaign, IL: Human Kinetics.

Elliott, D., Zuberec, S., & Milgrim, P. (1994). The effects of periodic visual occlusion on ball catching. *Journal of Motor Behavior, 26,* 113-122.

Schmidt, R.A., & Lee, T.D. (2011). Sensory contributions to motor control. In *Motor control and learning: A behavioral emphasis* (5th ed). (pp. 135-176). Champaign, IL: Human Kinetics.

Moving Sidewalks and Beer Glasses

How does the end-state comfort effect influence movement planning?

The next time you go to a restaurant with empty water glasses on the table, pay special attention to how the server fills them. Take note of how your glass is sitting on the table; some restaurants (such as outdoor cafés) have the glass overturned. If the server is holding a pitcher of water in one hand, watch very closely what she does with the other hand as she reaches for the glass. Quite likely, the server will pick up the glass with an inverted hand position, then turn both the hand and the glass over so she can pour water into the glass that she is now holding in a comfortable hand position.

This simple observation started psychologist David Rosenbaum on a long research journey, conducting many elegant studies along the way about how we plan actions prior to movement. His observations and initial research efforts were described simply as the end-state comfort effect. The idea is that we adopt initial body postures (e.g., hand configurations) in a highly predictable manner: we sacrifice efficiency and effectiveness initially to conclude the action in a comfortable final body posture.

The end-state comfort effect occurs because we anticipate a potentially awkward final posture and make adjustments ahead of time to minimize the discomfort. Another example of this phenomenon occurs in airports. Many airports contain moving sidewalks to transport people and their luggage. Getting on and off these moving sidewalks, however, causes a disturbance to our normal posture: getting on them causes us to fall backward, and getting off them causes us to fall forward. People who fly frequently have learned to anticipate what will happen when they get on and off these moving sidewalks. To minimize the disturbance, they make adjustments in their posture just before stepping on or off the sidewalk. Perhaps they do this not just to maximize their end-state comfort but also to minimize their chances of injury.

Now consider the task of putting away beer glasses. Pilsner beer glasses are tall and thin and can be grasped at a number of locations near the middle, top, or bottom of the glass. Suppose you were putting pilsner glasses away in the cupboard and had to put some on shelves that were above your head and some on shelves that were below your waist. Rosenbaum's research suggests that you would probably grasp the bottom of the glass if you were placing one in a high cupboard and grasp the top of the glass if placing one on a low shelf to avoid having to reach higher or lower than necessary. This illustrates the end-state comfort rules again.

Now suppose that just after you placed these glasses on their respective shelves, I ask you to bring each glass back to the countertop. It stands to reason from the end-state comfort effect that because you are placing both glasses on the same spot on the countertop (i.e., the same end-state position), your initial hand position on the glass would be the same, perhaps somewhere near the middle. Instead, Rosenbaum found that his participants did not perform as expected. When asked to immediately replace an object, Rosenbaum's participants adopted a hand position that was similar to the grasp used just moments ago. In other words, a memory effect took precedence over the end-state comfort effect.

These studies, elegant in their design yet simple in methodology, suggest that actions are planned on the basis of various strategies. The reasons for acting spontaneously to maximize our end-state comfort are pretty straightforward: effectiveness, efficiency, and injury prevention probably all play important roles. The reasons for a memory effect are much less clear, however, and research continues to uncover the effects and roles of recent memory in our moment-to-moment actions. Both effects, however, show a powerful effect of memory: both recollective memory (of the recent past) and prospective memory (for activities to occur in the future) influence our present behavior.

SELF-DIRECTED LEARNING ACTIVITIES

1. Explain the end-state comfort effect in your own words.
2. Describe two other activities of daily living in which the end-state comfort effect determines motor behavior.
3. Describe another activity in which recent memory of a previous action plays a dominant role in how the action is repeated.
4. Develop a research methodology to explore the maximizing of end-state comfort when passing objects from one hand to the other or from one person to another.

NOTES

- Noting that David Rosenbaum's experiments are simple is certainly not intended to be a slight to his research. Just the opposite is true: his experiments are simple in their methods, elegant in their design, and complex in their implications.
- David Rosenbaum's website describes some of his most recent research activities:
  http://cls.psu.edu/people/affiliated/rosenbaum_david.shtml

SUGGESTED READINGS

Rosenbaum, D.A., Loukopoulos, L.D., Meulenbroek, R.G.M., Vaughan, J., & Engelbrecht, S.E. (1995). Planning reaches by evaluating stored postures. *Psychological Review, 102,* 28-67.

Schmidt, R.A., & Lee, T.D. (2011). Human information processing. In *Motor control and learning: A behavioral emphasis* (5th ed., pp. 57-96) Champaign, IL: Human Kinetics.

Weigelt, M., Cohen, R.G., & Rosenbaum, D.A. (2007). Returning home: Locations rather than movements are recalled in human object manipulation. *Experimental Brain Research, 149,* 191-198.

How do motor commands influence sensory feedback during motor control?

Most people have spots on their bodies that are highly sensitive and respond to the external stimulation of tickling. Some people laugh and giggle; others find it irritating. But, why is it that we can't tickle ourselves? Go ahead and try it. Why do you not get the same response when you do it that you get when someone else does it?

Here is another curiosity. Use the tip of your index finger and gently nudge your eyeball by pushing lightly against the skin at the corner of the eye. What you will probably see is that the visual world jumps around when your eyeball is nudged; vision is blurred, and fixating on any one target becomes difficult. Now, instead of moving your eyeball with your finger, just quickly dart your eyes around, stopping very briefly to fixate on something. Notice that, in this case, your vision was not blurred.

Both of the preceding examples are classic demonstrations of an important capability of the central nervous system to interpret sensation. These examples demonstrate the capability for feedback cancellation (or, perhaps more precisely, feedback attenuation). *Feedback* refers the sensory information that arises as the result of movement. In some cases that sensory information has arisen because of something that we have done ourselves, and in other cases, it has arisen because of some other source. In all cases the attenuation of feedback occurs when we are expecting something specific to happen. For example, the sensation of a sudden and rapid acceleration in a car is not the same for the driver as it is for an unsuspecting passenger. For the driver, the rapid acceleration is a predictable result of having just pressed down hard on the accelerator. For the unaware passenger, however, who does not have such predictive knowledge of the change in the speed of the car, the sensation that arises from the feedback information is greatly heightened. Being prepared for a sensation that is about to occur changes how we experience that sensation once it does occur.

One of the remarkable features of our motor control system is the capability to predict the results of our intentions—in terms of both the expected outcome of our actions and the exact feedback sensations. This is not something that we have to try to do; it is a natural consequence of actively moving about in our environment. Sensory awareness is reduced, or attenuated, when the actual sensations match the predicted sensations. Perhaps this attenuation process is a way for the body to reduce the amount

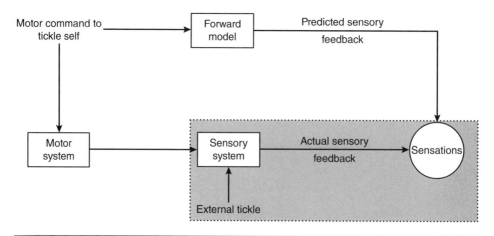

Figure 7.3   A model of sensations arising from self- and external tickles.

of sensory information we would have to deal with if everything that occurred as the result of our actions were completely unpredicted.

A model of the processes involved in tickling is presented in figure 7.3. According to researchers such as Sarah Blakemore, the process of trying to tickle yourself produces a set of anticipated signals that would be expected to arise from our skin receptors via the peripheral nervous system. Those signals change how we interpret the actual signals, drastically altering the tickling sensation. In contrast, the section of figure 7.3 highlighted in gray illustrates what happens when someone else tickles us. In this case, the absence of self-generated motor commands allows us to experience the sensation of the tickle without the attenuation of expected sensory feedback.

Of considerable interest, however, is that Blakemore and her colleagues found that the ticklish feeling can be partially reestablished if a temporal delay is inserted between your motor commands to tickle and the sensation arising from those motor commands. To do this, the researchers used a robotic "tickle machine" that provided the tickles after varying delays. In relation to the components illustrated in figure 7.3, the fidelity of the expected sensory feedback has been reduced by the time shift between the motor commands and the actual feedback. In other words, the feedback attenuation effect may depend on those sensory signals being received in a timely manner.

SELF-DIRECTED LEARNING ACTIVITIES

1. Define the term *feedback attenuation* in your own words.
2. Explain how the examples of pushing on your eyeball and trying to tickle yourself relate to the model presented in figure 7.3.
3. How does the sensation of a needle injected into your arm relate to the model presented in figure 7.3?

4. Blakemore and colleagues used a self-controlled tickling machine (a robotic device) to control the time interval between the motor command to tickle and the response made by the machine. Describe a modification to this experimental technique that would help you understand more about the experience of tickling sensations.

NOTES

- Much of our current knowledge about forward models of movement control arose from the early work of Hermann von Helmholtz. This is a good starting point for more on this important researcher:
  http://plato.stanford.edu/entries/hermann-helmholtz/

SUGGESTED READINGS

Blakemore, S.-J., Wolpert, D.M., & Frith, C.D. (1998). Central cancellation of self-produced tickle sensation. *Nature Neuroscience, 1,* 635-640.

Blakemore, S.-J., Wolpert, D.M., & Frith, C.D. (2000). Why can't you tickle yourself? *Neuroreport, 11,* R11-R16.

Schmidt, R.A., & Lee, T.D. (2011). Central contributions to motor control. In *Motor control and learning: A behavioral emphasis* (5th ed., pp. 177-222) Champaign, IL: Human Kinetics.

Wolpert, D.M., & Flanagan, J.R. (2001). Motor prediction. *Current Biology, 11,* R729-R732.

Is there a point in time after which an initiated motor program cannot be stopped?

Steve Williams has caddied for Tiger Woods for many years, and on occasion, his actions have caused some controversy. In one instance, Williams went into a crowd of people who were watching Tiger hit a shot to take a camera away from a photographer who had snapped a picture in the middle of one of Tiger's swings. Such a disruption would normally be infuriating to a professional golfer, but Tiger calmly stopped his downswing, backed away from the shot, and started over again. How did he do that?

What Tiger demonstrated is something that we actually see fairly often in sports other than golf. In baseball batting, for example, the decision to swing is based on the perceived "hit-ability" of a pitch, which is gathered from the flow of information about the oncoming ball flight (see "Preventing Penalties and Batting Baseballs" in chapter 5). Sometimes the visual information received early in the pitch would indicate that the ball is very hit-able, so the batter initiates a swing. But later visual information tells the batter that the earlier decision was wrong and that now would be a good time to change that decision and not swing.

The checked swing in baseball (see figure 7.4a) is an illustration of a successful reversal in the decision to act. Like Tiger, the batter initiated the trigger to swing but then initiated a second "stop swing" signal that was effective in arresting the swing before it was too late. The rules of baseball, however, define very clearly when the batter has been successful in checking a swing. If that internal signal to stop the swing is not sent soon enough, the bat will cross the plate and the umpire will rule that the batter has swung at the pitch (see figure 7.4b). The batter's success in checking the swing before the bat crosses the top of the plate is very likely a matter of time: the second signal (to stop the swing) must be sent very soon after the first signal (to start the swing) to have any chance of inhibiting it.

The Tiger Woods example and the checked swing in baseball raise a number of fascinating questions about motor control. Is there a point of no return once an action has been started? Is there a point in time after which the full execution of the action can no longer be stopped? If so, is there something in particular about the nature of the action or the person who is performing the action that makes it unstoppable?

Before we can begin to answer questions about how a batter might stop a baseball swing, let's review a couple of findings about what might underlie

a

b

Figure 7.4 The checked swing in baseball: *(a)* successful, *(b)* unsuccessful. At what point must the batter make the decision to reverse the earlier decision to swing at the pitch? What is the point of no return?

Figure 7.4*a*: Steven King/Icon SMI
Figure 7.4*b*: Frank Jansky/Icon SMI

the swing in the first place. For this, we call upon the concept of a motor program and what role it might play in the initiation of an action.

One clue about the role of a motor program in movement initiation comes from experiments on the subjective estimate of time. In this research the subjects' task was to simply watch the second hand of an analog clock sweep around the clockface and to press a button at any time. Immediately after pressing the button, the subjects estimated the point on the clockface where the clock hand had been when they pressed the button. Even given this very simple task, most subjects believed that the clock hand position was at an earlier point than it actually was when they pressed the button. Why did they make this consistent error bias in such a simple, voluntary task?

One leading argument is that this subjective error reflects the dissociation between the initiation of the motor program and the action resulting from initiating the motor program. The error occurs because the subject misattributes the command to release the motor program to the actual start of the movement itself. Hence, the belief is that the point on the clock when the button was pressed is actually the point on the clock when the motor program to press the button was sent to the muscles.

In an earlier story ("Antilock Brakes" in chapter 5) I discussed the research of Franklin Henry, who found evidence for the existence of motor programs that underlie the control of more complex, rapid actions. In his work Henry found that the time delay in initiating a motor program was directly related to the complexity of the action to be performed and, theoretically, directly related to the complexity of the motor program underlying it. Given this finding, it is quite reasonable to suspect that there should be an even longer delay before the initiation of a movement that is under the control of a more complex motor program (such as a baseball swing) than before a simple button press.

The point of all this is that initiating an action takes time because of the underlying neural activity that must occur before a movement can actually begin. For the result of a movement to occur at a specific point in time (such as hitting a baseball), the temporal delays in getting the action started must be anticipated and factored into the timing of the entire action, as well as the time that it takes for the movement to be completed.

Now consider how much time is needed to stop a motor program after it has been initiated. One clue to answer that question came from some research by Arthur Slater-Hammel many years ago, which in some ways mimicked the checked swing situation. Participants in his study were asked to perform an anticipation task by lifting a finger from a button when a rapidly rotating sweeping hand reached the 10 o'clock position (not unlike the anticipation timing required to swing a bat and hit a pitched ball as it crosses the plate). As suggested before, the subjects couldn't wait until the sweeping hand actually reached the 10 o'clock position before issuing the command to lift the finger because of the delays in the initiation and execution of the motor program, as well as in making the movement itself. The command to start the motor program needed to be sent well in advance of the coincident point.

This being a simple task, Slater-Hammel's subjects quickly figured it out and were stopping the sweep hand at close to the 10 o'clock position. A critical point in the experiment occurred, however, when Slater-Hammel introduced a catch trial into the sequence of normal trials, in which the clock automatically stopped on its own, prior to the 10 o'clock position. The participants were instructed that whenever a catch trial occurred, they were to try to stop themselves from lifting their finger. Essentially, this is the same as the checked swing in baseball (if the batter sees that the pitch is out of the strike zone, he must stop himself from completing the initiated swing). For these catch trials, the important measure of performance was whether or not the subjects were successful in inhibiting their response. Again, this is similar to the baseball situation because success would be measured in terms of whether or not the batter successfully checked the swing (see figure 7.4).

Slater-Hammel found that his participants were successful in preventing their finger from releasing the button only if the clock hand stopped more than 200 milliseconds before the 10 o'clock position. For positions less than 160 milliseconds or so from 10 o'clock position, the participants could not stop themselves from lifting their finger. It was as if the control of the finger had been turned over to the motor program responsible for its execution, and once the program had been initiated, the participant no longer had control over the finger's action.

The implications of these results are complicated by the fact that the baseball swing is a much more complex action than the simple finger lift in Slater-Hammel's study. The finger lift is very much a ballistic action, and the motor program to initiate it is probably also very simple. The baseball swing, on the other hand, has a longer movement time and more complex motor program underlying it, which produces some advantages and disadvantages. The bad news is that the swing would need to be initiated well before a comparable finger lift because of the added movement time involved in getting the bat into the hitting area and the added initiation time involved in recruiting a more complex motor program. The good news is that this additional delay would also provide more time for the batter to change the decision to swing. As a result, the checked swing in baseball is not an either–or situation, and we sometimes see the batter check the swing before the bat starts to move, sometimes just before it crosses the plate, or sometimes not until after the bat has crossed the plate.

Numerous lines of evidence suggest that motor programs exist and that they play an important role in the control and alteration of intended actions. But, is there a point of no return—a point in time when the action cannot be modified at all? One more finding, provided by Gordon Logan, helps to answer this question. Logan asked skilled typists to type prose in a normal way, but to stop typing whenever an auditory signal was presented. He found that the typists could stop very quickly when they heard the signal, suggesting that a point of no return does not exist. However, there was one exception: the typists could not stop typing the word *the* before the entire word (including the space after the word) had been typed. One interpretation of this result was that a highly overlearned motor program for *the_* had been developed in these typists, the full execution of which was nearly impossible to inhibit once it had been initiated. For *the_*, initiation of the uninterruptible motor program represented a point of no return.

So, what we have is a rather complex set of findings. On the one hand, a highly overlearned motor program for typing seems to control the execution of an entire coordinated action once initiated. On the other hand, complex movements such as the golf and the baseball swing seem to be modifiable well after they have begun. For highly skilled typists, the development of a motor program for typing the word *the* appears to have developed with practice. For highly skilled baseball players and golfers, the ability to modify a well-learned action may be a consequence of learning, too. The reasons for these discrepancies are not well understood and remain an impetus for future research.

SELF-DIRECTED LEARNING ACTIVITIES

1. Explain the point of no return in your own words.
2. Suggest another highly overlearned word or phrase that might represent an unmodifiable motor program in skilled typists.
3. A checked swing in baseball occurs when a batter cancels a previously initiated motor program. Suggest a different activity in which the motor program is not canceled, but instead is replaced with a different motor program.
4. Suggest a methodology for studying the time to check the swing in baseball using the methods Slater-Hammel used.

NOTES

- Important biomechanical influences are involved in successfully checking the baseball swing, such as arresting the angular momentum and torque in the swing.

SUGGESTED READINGS

Gray, R. (2009). A model of motor inhibition for a complex skill: Baseball batting. *Journal of Experimental Psychology: Applied, 15,* 91-105.

Logan, G.D. (1982). On the ability to inhibit complex movements: A stop-signal study of typewriting. *Journal of Experimental Psychology: Human Perception and Performance, 8,* 778-792.

Schmidt, R.A., & Lee, T.D. (2011). Central contributions to motor control. In *Motor control and learning: A behavioral emphasis* (5th ed., pp. 177-222) Champaign, IL: Human Kinetics.

Slater-Hammel, A.T. (1960). Reliability, accuracy and refractoriness of a transit reaction. *Research Quarterly, 31,* 217-228.

What are generalized motor programs, and what do keystroke dynamics reveal about them?

Most of what I know about forensic identification comes from crime shows that I've seen on TV. The suspect is caught because a fingerprint was left on the murder weapon. The evidence is used to convict the suspect because no two fingerprints have ever been found to be identical. Crime shows tell us that other forensic methods can be used as well, such as DNA and eye retina data, but the fingerprint is the oldest biometric tool used for identification. However, another method that reveals a great deal about your identity is how you write or even type your name. For example, the password that you type to log on to your e-mail account may be just as identifiable as your fingerprint.

Try the following task as an example: go into any word processing program and type your name 10 times, once on each line, as I have done here:

Tim Lee

Tim Lee

Tim Lee

Tim Lee

Tim Lee

Tim Lee

Tim Lee

Tim Lee

Tim Lee

Tim Lee

I am not a skilled typist. I use my right middle finger to hold down the shift key and press the letter *T* with my left middle finger, then use my right middle finger to press *i* and my right index finger to press *m*, and then my right thumb to press the space bar. It is not very efficient, but I do it the same way every time I type my name. Regardless of how skilled a typist you are, you most likely repeat much the same process each of the 10 times you type your name.

Now, let's try to unravel the temporal "fingerprint" that you left behind when you typed your name. Suppose we conducted a simple analysis of the keystrokes and the time between each of the keystrokes that you made. The total time taken to type your name once is simply the time from the first keystroke to the last keystroke. At a more fine-grained level of analysis, the total time constitutes the time each key is held down (the dwell time) plus the time between the release of one key and the depression of the next (the transition time). All of the individual dwell times plus all of the transition times will sum to the total time.

In figure 7.5, I have plotted a hypothetical example of the 10 trials to type my name. The light gray bands denote the dwell times, and the darker gray bands indicate the transition times. I have ordered the lines of bands that represent the 10 trials from the fastest (least total time) at the top to the slowest trial at the bottom (most total time).

If you were to analyze each of the 10 repetitions of your name, you would probably find that all of the total times would be similar, but probably never *exactly* the same each time, just as in figure 7.5. The "noise" in our central nervous systems, plus other factors, causes the results to vary a little bit each time, resulting in some repetitions to be slower, and others faster, than the average total time.

But, take a closer look at each individual band in figure 7.5 as it changes over the 10 trials. What you will notice is that as the total time increases, each band gets proportionally longer too. We could express these numbers another way by dividing the time for each individual band by the total time for that trial to obtain a relative proportion of time represented by each band. Given the hypothetical evidence in figure 7.5, what we would discover is that the relative time for each band, expressed as a percentage, would stay roughly the same across all of the repetitions. Applying temporal and other methods to deconstruct how we type (e.g., key press forces) is called the study of keystroke dynamics.

According to generalized motor program theory, relative time is one of the key features of movement that is controlled by the central nervous system,

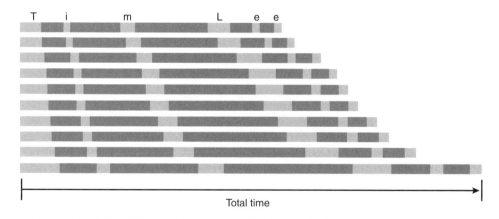

Figure 7.5   Ten hypothetical trials for typing my name. Each trial is represented as a single horizontal line, with the fastest trial (shortest total time) at the top and the slowest trial (longest total time) at the bottom.

especially for brief, rapid actions. Relative time is an expression of our motor control fingerprint. For well-learned tasks such as typing and handwriting, our central nervous system regulates the relative timing of impulses that are sent to the muscles that carry out these tasks. Various factors influence the real time on any particular instance. For example, using a keyboard that requires more force to depress the keys might result in overall slower times than would result using a keyboard that has a light touch, but the relative timing would likely remain the same.

Research in keystroke dynamics may result in the ability to identify people who carry out Internet fraud. In many ways it is similar to the use of handwriting dynamics to analyze the timing of the cursive expressions of a signature. It is fairly easy to forge the spatial representation of someone's signature, but very difficult to forge the temporal dynamics that result in that signature. These expressions of timing behavior represent our motor control fingerprints.

SELF-DIRECTED LEARNING ACTIVITIES

1. Define the term *generalized motor program* in your own words.

2. How does the concept of a generalized motor program differ from the concept of a motor program as it was used in stories such as "Antilock Brakes" (in chapter 5) and "Point of No Return" (earlier in this chapter)?

3. Suggest a method by which the handwriting dynamics of signatures could be used to detect fraud.

4. Some people contend that there is one generalized motor program for the full swing in golf, regardless of which club is used. How could a temporal dynamics analysis be used to assess this contention?

NOTES

- An excellent review of fingerprint analysis by David Ashbaugh of the Royal Canadian Mounted Police is available here:

    www.onin.com/fp/ridgeology.pdf

- A lot of controversy remains about invariances in motor performance; how they are measured; and what invariance, or lack of invariance, means in terms of motor programs. The following articles provide good arguments for the debate:

    Gentner, D.R. (1987). Timing of skilled motor performance: Tests of the proportional duration model. *Psychological Review, 94,* 255-276.

    Heuer, H. (1988). Testing the invariance of relative timing: Comment on Gentner (1987). *Psychological Review, 95,* 552-557.

SUGGESTED READINGS

Schmidt, R.A. (1975). A schema theory of discrete motor skill learning. *Psychological Review, 82,* 225-260.

Schmidt, R.A. (1985). The search for invariance in skilled movement behavior. *Research Quarterly for Exercise and Sport, 56,* 188-200.

Schmidt, R.A., & Lee, T.D. (2011). Central contributions to motor control. In *Motor control and learning: A behavioral emphasis* (5th ed., pp. 177-222) Champaign, IL: Human Kinetics.

How does the nervous system use functional linkages to coordinate movements?

Everybody knows the coordination task in which you try to pat your head and rub your belly at the same time. Here is another one that was going around the Internet a few years ago: While sitting in a chair, lift your foot slightly off the floor and make it go around in small clockwise circles. While your foot is circling use the index finger of your right hand to draw the number 6 in the air. If you are like most people, your right foot will switch directions and start to go in the same direction as your hand. The feeling is most bizarre—it is almost as if some other force has taken over control of your foot.

The issue concerns the problem of coordination—how your central nervous system deals with the task of controlling two or more body segments that are moving at the same time. The steering mechanism of a typical car provides an analogy that helps to understand the solution to the problem (see figure 7.6). The car moves in a direction that is specified by the two front wheels. And yet, we don't have to think about the direction that each wheel is headed because they are linked together with the steering column: you

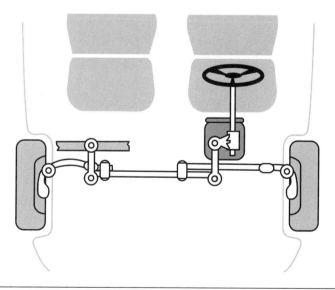

Figure 7.6 The car steering system is a good example of controlling two degrees of freedom (the direction of each front wheel) by reducing to one degree of freedom (controlled by the movements of the steering wheel).

move the steering wheel, which causes the steering column to rotate, which in turn causes both front wheels to move by the same amount. The front wheels have a fixed linkage, meaning that any movement of the steering wheel will result in identical changes in both the right and left front wheels. Imagine how different and more difficult the task of steering a car would be if you had separate controls for each wheel!

The steering system reduces the degrees of freedom involved in steering from two to one by means of the fixed linkage. It has solved the problem of coordinating the independently moving two wheels by removing their independence. Our motor control system also has many independently moving parts—degrees of freedom that might otherwise present a problem for us to coordinate if we did not have a central nervous system that provides us with linkages that are both functional and flexible. One of the remarkable features of human movement is that we can achieve the same result using very different routes to success (see "Websites and Silly Walks").

Take, for example, the task of maintaining balance when standing on a bus or a subway. Suppose you are facing the front of the vehicle when it quickly comes to a stop. The physics of bringing the vehicle to a stop naturally propels your body forward. How do you maintain your balance? Research by Horak and Nashner revealed that we use one of three strategies to maintain or regain balance (illustrated in figure 7.7). Two of the strategies (the left and middle illustrations in figure 7.7) are used to maintain or regain postural stability by making postural adjustments about the ankle or hip, without changing the base of support. The third strategy (right side of figure 7.7) uses a step to stop the forward momentum of our body sway.

Let's consider just the first two strategies for now. Both involve a collective functional linkage of muscles that span a joint, either the ankle or hip, to bring balance under control. And both use an entirely different set of linkages to do so. This example nicely illustrates how the body organizes a set of degrees of freedom to work together to achieve a common goal, but also illustrates that we are not forced to use an inflexible linkage to do so. We can solve the problem without moving our feet in two very different but effective ways—by invoking either the ankle or hip strategy.

These and many other studies of controlling multiple degrees of freedom at the same time reveal that acts of coordination are sometimes easy and sometimes more difficult to do. Here is another demonstration, provided by researcher Scott Kelso. Shape your hands like two pistols and hold them in front of you, as if you were about to shoot at a target. Now start to rhythmically wiggle just the right index finger back and forth. After a few seconds of wiggling just the right finger start wiggling the left index finger too. Look to see what pattern the two index fingers spontaneously adopt. When I ask the students in my class to do this, almost everyone in the class moves the fingers toward each other and then away from each other. This is called moving in an in-phase pattern and is probably spontaneously adopted because it is the most natural and comfortable timing pattern to use in this

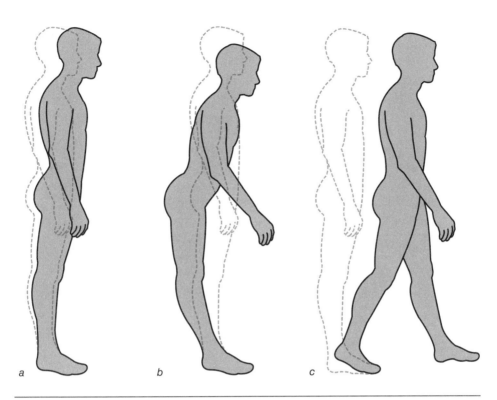

a   b   c

Figure 7.7   Balance control strategies: *(a)* ankle strategy; *(b)* hip strategy; *(c)* step strategy.

situation. Note that there is no fixed linkage that requires the fingers to coordinate in this manner. Rather, the fingers are spontaneously linked to engage in a pattern that allows both fingers to move simultaneously, with little effort or attention required to keep each of them under control. Instead of a fixed linkage, the central nervous system has created a movement pattern, or functional linkage, that allows the timing of two separate body segments to be controlled as easily as one segment.

Although we spontaneously tend to adopt an in-phase pattern in this case, as intentionally acting human beings with functional linkages, we are not compelled to wiggle our fingers in just this one pattern, as the two front wheels of a car are compelled to do. Hold your pistols out again but now move them in the same direction. That is, move both index fingers to the right, then to the left, then right, and so on, which is called moving in an antiphase pattern. This pattern (used by many automakers in their windshield wiper fixed linkage systems) is also an easy one to maintain. The flexibility of the central nervous system has permitted us the functional capacity to move in either an in-phase or antiphase pattern with relative ease.

But these are not the only patterns that we can use to simultaneously wiggle our fingers. In fact, with practice we can learn to perform essentially any one of an infinite number of timing patterns for these two degrees of freedom, of which only two patterns are inherently simple to produce. And, some people can actually move a foot in clockwise circles while writing the number 6 with the index finger. They have managed to overcome the tendency of the central nervous system to coordinate these two moving segments in the most natural functional linkage—that is, moving both in the same direction. Achieving each separate goal while moving both limbs at the same time has been achieved because of practice. A new functional linkage has been learned that allows this pattern of foot and hand movements to be performed together with ease and efficiency. They have solved a puzzle that requires motor learning. Lots more is said about learning in part III of this book.

SELF-DIRECTED LEARNING ACTIVITIES

1. Define the term *degrees of freedom* in your own words.
2. How does a linkage change the degrees of freedom in performing a task?
3. Explain the difference between a fixed linkage and a functional linkage.
4. Design and conduct an experiment in which a person sits in an elevated chair and swings one upper limb and one lower limb at the same time. What natural functional linkages do you find?

NOTES

- The trick of the foot and tracing the number 6 will work only if you make your 6s starting at the top and going in a counterclockwise direction.
- Controlling many independently moving parts at the same time is called the degrees of freedom problem; it was first described by the Russian scientist Nikolai Bernstein in the 1930s.

SUGGESTED READINGS

Horak, F.B., & Nashner, L.M. (1986). Central programming of postural movements: Adaptation to altered support surface configurations. *Journal of Neurophysiology, 55,* 1369-1381.

Kelso, J.A.S. (1984). Phase transitions and critical behavior in human bimanual coordination. *American Journal of Physiology: Regulatory, Integrative and Comparative Physiology, 15,* R1000-R1004.

Kelso, J.A.S. (1995). *Dynamic patterns: The self-organization of brain and behavior.* Cambridge, MA: MIT Press.

Schmidt, R.A., & Lee, T.D. (2011). Coordination. In *Motor control and learning: A behavioral emphasis* (5th ed., pp. 263-296) Champaign, IL: Human Kinetics.

What makes some coordination patterns more automatic than others?

In "Party Tricks," I asked you to form pistols with your two hands and move your index fingers rhythmically in either an in-phase or an antiphase pattern. Both patterns are easy to do and require no practice to perform effectively and efficiently. Now I want you to try something different. Using your finger pistols again, start moving in an in-phase pattern at a slow pace—say, one full cycle per second (1 Hz). Then slowly start to pick up the pace, gradually going faster and faster. You will find that it is rather easy to maintain the in-phase pattern. Now try the same thing beginning with the antiphase pattern at a slow speed, then gradually going faster and faster. If you perform like the students who do this in my classes, then at some point you will probably find that the antiphase pattern becomes more difficult to maintain; the stability of the pattern starts to fall apart. But something very interesting happens as the fingers are wiggled still faster and faster. Rather than the antiphase pattern completely disappearing into two randomly waving pistols, the pattern tends to be replaced by the in-phase pattern.

As was discussed in "Party Tricks," we have the capacity to move just these two simple degrees of freedom in an infinite number of independent ways. The in-phase and antiphase patterns appear to represent the most natural of this infinite repertoire of patterns. Moreover, when speed becomes a factor, we find that the in-phase pattern is the dominant solution, at least for this finger-wiggling task.

So, what is going on here? Several views have been forwarded, and each appears to be supported by research. According to one view, the coordination of multiple degrees of freedom is not directed by conscious intentions, as might be expected if commanded by the brain, as in a motor programming point of view. Instead, these patterns emerge, dissolve, and reformulate spontaneously depending on the self-organizing properties of the central nervous system and how the limbs interact with the environment and other conditions. According to this view, the decision about which pattern will dominate depends largely on how the general intentions of the performer interact with the self-organizing properties of the central nervous system.

An alternative view of these disappearing patterns is that they represent varying levels of learning, each associated with different attentional demand requirements (see "Gumbo" in chapter 6). In-phase and antiphase patterns can be performed while walking, while talking, and while walking *and* talking.

Researchers sometimes refer to actions of this type as automatic because they demand little or no attention for successful completion. The in-phase pattern appears to be consistent with the performance characteristics that we might expect from an automated pattern. It can be performed at very rapid speeds or together with other activities with little to no loss in performance capacity. In comparison, the antiphase pattern is less compatible with this view of automaticity: the pattern can be maintained only with increased attention at higher speeds or when combined with other activities, and even at that, performance will deteriorate. The tendency of the in-phase pattern to dominate the antiphase pattern is also consistent with the idea that we "regress" to a more highly learned, more automatic mode of control when placed in situations that push us to the edge of our performance capabilities.

A strikingly similar finding occurs in the control of gait. The two most common gaits in humans are walking and running, which propel us at different speeds. If we start walking at a slow speed and gradually walk faster and faster, we will want to switch to a running gait at about 4.7 miles per hour (2.1 m/s). Similarly, if we start running at a rapid pace and then go slower and slower, there will be a temptation to switch to a walking gait at roughly the same speed. The point at which this occurs is different for people of different shapes and sizes, but the transition is a natural response to increased energy demands because the gait we are using is no longer optimized for locomotion at that speed. However, if we intentionally continue to walk faster (or run slower) at speeds beyond the normal transition point, we will experience an increased variability in stride frequency and length.

The dissolution and reformation of coordination patterns reveals something quite interesting about the central nervous system. Although there is a tendency to associate variability with an increased likelihood of errors or accidents (e.g., see "The Calculator" and "The Gimme Putt" in chapter 3), this is not always the case. What we have discussed here is that the variability and error in the performance of certain patterns increase only when we intentionally try to resist a switch to a pattern that is better suited for the changed conditions (e.g., resisting the switch from antiphase to in-phase when moving faster and faster). Instead, when we let patterns dissolve and reformulate as new patterns, reductions in error are likely to occur. The conscious decision to resist the pattern dissolution is what results in the increased error. It seems as though sometimes our bodies are smarter than we are.

SELF-DIRECTED LEARNING ACTIVITIES

1. What does pattern switching refer to in the context of movement coordination?
2. How does an energy demand view of locomotion coordination differ from an attention demand view?

3. In the example, the antiphase coordination pattern disappeared and was replaced by an in-phase pattern as movement speeds increased. Why don't we start hopping when we run faster and faster?

4. Suppose, during the performance of a finger-wiggling task, you intentionally tried to switch from an in-phase pattern to an antiphase pattern (and vice versa). Which would be more difficult to do? How would you conduct such an experiment, and what measure of switching performance would provide the best indication of the relative difficulty of these two intentional switches?

NOTES

- The switch from an antiphase pattern to an in-phase pattern is not obligatory at high speeds, but must be counteracted intentionally to fight the attraction to an in-phase pattern, as discussed in the following studies:

    Lee, T.D., Blandin, Y., & Proteau, L. (1996). Effects of task instructions and oscillation frequency on bimanual coordination. *Psychological Research, 59,* 100-106.

    Smethurst, C.J., & Carson, R.G. (2003). The effect of volition on the stability of bimanual coordination. *Journal of Motor Behavior, 35,* 309-319.

- Changing gait patterns in four-legged animals is another fascinating area of research and reveals that some animals switch among five or six gait patterns, and do so for varying reasons. The following references are essential reading in this area:

    Hoyt, D.F., & Taylor, C.R. (1981). Gait and the energetics of locomotion in horses. *Science, 292,* 239-240.

    Alexander, R.M. (2003). *Principles of animal locomotion.* Princeton, NJ: Princeton University Press.

SUGGESTED READINGS

Diedrich, F.J., & Warren, W.H. Jr. (1995). Why change gaits? Dynamics of the walk-run transition. *Journal of Experimental Psychology: Human Perception and Performance, 21,* 183-202.

Diedrich, F.J., & Warren, W.H. Jr. (1998). Dynamics of human gait transitions. In D.A. Rosenbaum & C.E. Collyer (Eds.), *Timing of behavior: Neural, psychological, and computational perspectives* (pp. 323-343). Cambridge, MA: MIT.

Kelso, J.A.S., Scholz, J.P., & Schöner, G. (1986). Nonequilibrium phase transitions in coordinated biological motion: Critical fluctuations. *Physics Letters A, 118,* 279-284.

Schmidt, R.A., & Lee, T.D. (2011). Coordination. In *Motor control and learning: A behavioral emphasis* (5th ed., pp. 263-296). Champaign, IL: Human Kinetics.

PART THREE

STORIES ABOUT LEARNING MOTOR SKILLS

Most of us sign our names and make handwritten notes without giving the process of writing much thought. However, suppose I asked you to pick up a pen with your nondominant hand and use it to sign your name or make a shopping list. The simple process of handwriting has now become a challenge. You have to stop and think about how to hold the pen; your hand movements are slow, jerky, and unpredictable; and the results that appear on the paper may be difficult even for you to read. And yet, the same brain is being used with either task, and you have a clear mental picture of what the signature and words should look like when you are done. So, what's the problem?

Motor learning concerns the process by which we improve the certainty with which we carry out actions and achieve intentions. Researchers have studied the learning process for many years, and the techniques, paradigms, and tasks they have chosen to undertake these investigations are as varied as the actions they have sought to understand. The stories in part III provide a flavor of this research and the sometimes surprising discoveries that have resulted from many of these investigations.

CHAPTER EIGHT

MEASURING MOTOR LEARNING

To this point in the book, I have dealt with some issues for which the evidence and the concepts are relatively straightforward. We know that people slow down to reduce errors because of the evidence provided by time and error measurements (see "Pouring Coffee" in chapter 3). Accident rates skyrocket when drivers talk on cell phones, as revealed in evidence from both driver accident records and dual-task measures of performance in experiments (see "Gumbo" in chapter 6). I have also discussed concepts for which the evidence is circumstantial or argumentative at best. Reaction times increase as the nature of the task gets more complex, leading some to argue that a motor program underlies some types of performance (see "Antilock Brakes" in chapter 5). However, to my knowledge, nobody has ever really directly observed a motor program in action. Steve Nash is able to make a defender look bad by a well-timed fake, leading some to argue for the involvement of a refractory period (see "Fakes" in chapter 6). But again, the evidence for a psychological refractory period is not as rock solid as it is for physiological refractory periods. Some of these concepts require an accumulation of evidence from a variety of tasks, methods, experiments, and behavioral and physiological measures to strengthen the conclusions.

The study of motor learning often requires us to make a further set of inferences. In addition to making the same inferences as before, researchers must also try to understand how and why these processes change as a function of practice or experience. So, the first step to understanding research about motor learning is acquiring some grounding in the fundamentals of how the research is conducted. The most fundamental feature of learning is the basis for the story "How You Get to Carnegie Hall," but this feature is also one of the least understood by learners who are trying to find their own Carnegie Hall. "The Babe" takes a statistical look at what makes up an all-around athlete. One of the greatest golfers of her generation just might turn out to be Michelle Wie, although she has received a tremendous amount of criticism for the way she tried to improve her skills, the fairness of which we consider in "Learning to Win From Losing." I argue that many of the criticisms were based on faulty logic because they failed to consider the fundamental difference between performance and learning. In "Zero-Sum Training," the adage of a penny saved is a penny earned is used to explain the impact of poor practice methods. They are twice as bad as you might think.

How You Get to Carnegie Hall

What is the best way to measure progress in motor learning?

The old joke goes something like this: A visitor to New York City was hurriedly trying to find his way to Carnegie Hall to see the symphony. After a period of fruitless search, and fearing that he might miss the start of the concert, the visitor finally stopped a local resident and asked him, "How do I get to Carnegie Hall?" Without skipping a beat, the New Yorker replied, simply, "Practice, practice, practice."

The local resident was either joking with the visitor or had taken a course in motor learning, because nothing is more effective for improving motor skill than practice. But, not all forms of practice are created equal. We will see later that there are many ways to structure practice that will greatly influence the learning process. In general, however, the amount of practice is the single most important factor in the improvement of motor skills.

You may think that this is simply stating the obvious. But, the relationship between practice and the level of skill attained is not always one-to-one. Improvements in skill are sometimes quick. At other times, skill levels appear to stagnate, with no appreciable improvements, and indeed, may even seem to degrade for a period of time. And, sooner or later, learning may appear to have ended, with no more gains seemingly possible.

As an example, consider someone who is using chopsticks for the first time. With some helpful words of advice, or by watching others use their chopsticks, or both, the hungry learner can progress from complete novice to a very rudimentary level of skill proficiency in just one meal. This simple example illustrates that the most obvious and rapid improvements often occur in the earliest practice period when learning a new skill. Many of these performance improvements occur because of the acquisition of some fundamental techniques. In the case of using chopsticks, it may be because the learner has acquired information regarding which techniques of holding the chopsticks are effective and which are ineffective.

One way to quantify the gains in performance would be to measure the amount of food eaten in successive minutes. What we likely will find is that the novice chopsticks user eats very little in the first few minutes of a meal, but starts to enjoy the meal relatively quickly after these initial struggles. The classic shape of the performance acquisition graph is a negatively accelerating curve, as illustrated in figure 8.1. It is called negatively accelerating because the rapid gains in performance seen in the initial portions of the curve decelerate over time. Although the scores increase relative to the y-axis, the rate of change of these increases declines over time.

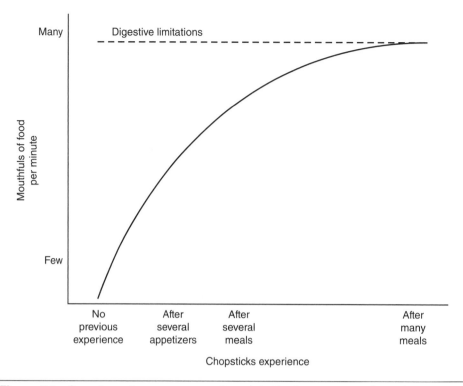

Figure 8.1   Sample performance curve that plots the improvement in performance in using chopsticks (as measured in mouthfuls of food eaten per minute) as a function of the amount of practice.

After some practice, perhaps a few meals or a few dozen meals later, the learner might have approached a maximum eating speed (because digestive factors limit how fast we can eat). In other words, the curve has leveled off, or reached a plateau. However, the leveling of the curve presents an interpretive problem. Does it mean that there is no room for further improvements in using chopsticks so that the learning is complete? The answer, of course, is no. Instead, the leveling of the curve simply means that our measure of skill (the amount of food eaten per minute) is no longer sensitive or appropriate for indexing further improvements in skill. This illustrates one of the important concepts in motor learning research—that the absence of further observable (or obvious) changes in performance does not mean that other aspects of performance are not continuing to improve. Most certainly, the dexterity and efficiency of using chopsticks continue to improve over the course of many, many meals.

But, how long might skills continue to improve? A study reported in Crossman (1959) suggests that, in fact, motor learning may never end. Crossman tracked the performance of cigar rollers over a seven-year period. His finding was that performance time continued to improve for years and only leveled off when the operational constraints of the machinery prevented further reductions in performance time (similar to the digestive limits in our chopsticks example).

In learning even relatively simple motor skills, such as using chopsticks, the observable actions reveal only some of the changes in the central nervous system that underlie the skill itself. Movement efficiency, repeatability, transferability of the skill to novel situations or objects, and the ability to perform the skill while multitasking are all examples of ways motor skills continue to improve. Regardless of what represents your Carnegie Hall, getting there is a matter of practice, practice, practice.

SELF-DIRECTED LEARNING ACTIVITIES

1. Define *motor learning* in your own words.
2. Look at figure 8.1 once again. How would the curve look if improvements in the measure of performance were revealed by a decreasing score (such as a smaller reaction time or a reduced error score)?
3. Figure 8.1 was described as a negatively accelerating curve. What would you call the curve that you conceptualized in question 2?
4. In the chopsticks example described in the story, the measure of performance (mouthfuls of food eaten) quickly became an inappropriate measure of learning. Suggest another measure of performance that would be more appropriate and sensitive to longer-term changes in the acquisition of chopsticks skill.

NOTE

- Directions to Carnegie Hall:
  www.tinyurl.com/directionscarnegie

SUGGESTED READINGS

Crossman, E.R.F.W. (1959). A theory of the acquisition of speed skill. *Ergonomics, 2,* 153-166.

Schmidt, R.A., & Lee, T.D. (2011). Motor learning concepts and research methods. In *Motor control and learning: A behavioral emphasis* (5th ed., pp. 327-346). Champaign, IL: Human Kinetics.

Can a general motor ability be defined and measured?

All sports considered, the Babe ranks as one of the greatest athletes of all time. You may be thinking that I am referring to the baseball legend George Herman "Babe" Ruth, who was also known as the Sultan of Swat, the Great Bambino, and the Home Run King—the guy who powered his way to 714 home runs using hotdogs and beer as his stimulants of choice, rather than amphetamines, steroids, or human growth hormones.

But, no. The Babe that I'm talking about is Mildred "Babe" (Didrikson) Zaharias, another legendary athlete. She did it all, and did it all very, very well. Here is a partial list of her accomplishments: she was a professional athlete in the sports of basketball, baseball, tennis, and bowling; won two gold medals and one silver medal in track and field at the 1932 Summer Olympics; and dominated women's golf at both the amateur and professional levels for two decades until her untimely death from cancer at the age of 45. Babe Zaharias was the quintessential all-around athlete.

But what does the term *all-around athlete* really mean? We all have known people like Babe Zaharias—the kids who starred on the football and basketball teams and won medals in track and field. On the other hand, at the opposite end of the spectrum were those other kids—the all-around *non*athletes. They seemed to have no proficiency in motor skills whatsoever. Is there a simple factor that accounts for the occurrence of these all-around athletes and nonathletes? A popular view, sometimes called the general motor ability view, was that all-around athletes possess a general capability for skilled motor performance; they are good at all kinds of sports because they have an exceptional general capacity to perform motor skills. Conversely, the all-around nonathletes lack this general capability for skilled performance. Not surprisingly, the general motor ability view shared many similarities with views about the generality of other skills, such as cognitive skills (or general intelligence). Cognitive skills represent a person's fundamental potential for intellectual aptitudes and are supposedly captured in terms of an overall, unitary value (such as an IQ score).

One of the pioneering motor control and learning researchers in kinesiology, Franklin Henry (see "Antilock Brakes" in chapter 5), reasoned that if the general motor ability concept were true, a simple statistical prediction could be expected. Specifically, he suggested that if the all-around athlete were someone with an exceptional general motor ability, then an outstanding athlete would reveal excellent performances on a variety of athletic measures. Similarly, a person of good general ability should perform reasonably well on all of the same motor tasks, the average athlete would perform about average on the tests, and so on, with the poor athlete performing very poorly on all of the motor tasks in a motor skills test battery. Specifically, Henry predicted that if, say, 100 people of all abilities were to perform two motor skills tests, it would be expected that the best athletes would rank highest on both tests, the average athletes would rank average on both tests, and the weak athletes would rank poorly on both tests. In other words, their performances would be as shown in figure 8.2.

A statistical analysis called a correlation coefficient (r) measures the degree of association between two sets of data, such as the correlation between the performances on one skills test and the performances on a second skills test. If the degree of association is extremely high, then the correlation coefficient will approach a maximum value of $r = 1.0$. Indeed, if the rank of all 100 athletes followed the trend illustrated in figure 8.2, then the correlation coefficient would be a perfect $r = 1.0$.

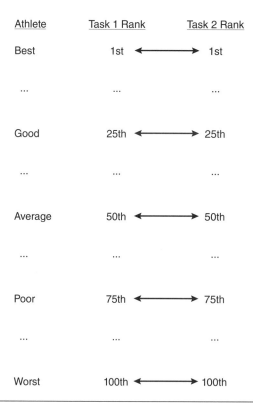

Figure 8.2 An illustration of the prediction made by the general motor ability view. In this view, a person's ranked position on a performance test should be similar in two motor tasks, especially if the motor tasks are relatively similar (e.g., two balance tasks). A correlation measure for the data represented in this figure would reveal a high degree of association between the performances in the two tasks.

Henry and his students performed a number of studies that compared motor skills performance using various forms of balance tasks, speed tasks, and other tests of motor performance. In fact, sometimes the two tasks that were compared were very similar, such as balancing on one foot versus two feet or comparing the speed of responding with a hand (reaction time) versus the speed of moving a hand to a target (movement time) (see "Red Light, Green Light" in chapter 5, for more on the differences between reaction and movement time). The results were nothing at all like those in figure 8.2. Instead, they found something like the results illustrated in figure 8.3. Henry and his students found the correlation coefficients to be near zero (*r* = 0.0).

These results, together with findings made by researchers in other laboratories, quite effectively refuted the general motor ability view. But, how does one explain the existence of a person like the Babe? Henry interpreted the findings of this research to suggest that the abilities that were responsible for a performance on any particular motor task are specific and unique to that task, and uncorrelated with the abilities required for the performance of a different task. In other words, Henry argued quite strongly that there is no general underlying motor ability. Instead, Henry suggested that people

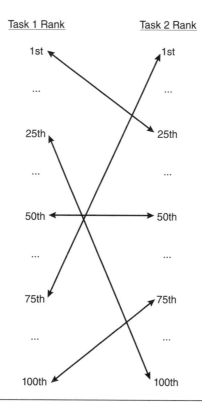

Figure 8.3 An illustration of the findings of the research conducted by Henry and his colleagues. Performance tests in two motor tasks revealed a very low degree of association, resulting in a correlation coefficient of near zero.

possess many separate abilities that are independent of one another and at very specific levels. In Henry's view, one's capacity to perform well on a task was a reflection of the level of abilities required to perform that task combined with the skills that have been practiced and are unique to that task. Therefore, the capacity to perform any one task will be specific because the requisite abilities and skills learned will be unique to that task. Hence, the relation between the performances on any two tasks will be uncorrelated.

Henry did not deny that athletes with a large number of exceptional motor abilities, like Babe Zaharias, existed. Moreover, someone like Zaharias, who probably devoted considerable practice time to each of her professional sports, could enhance her capacity to perform well with these specific abilities. But Henry denied that this evidence converged to support the view of athletic prowess as an expression of one single overarching motor ability.

SELF-DIRECTED LEARNING ACTIVITIES

1. Explain the general motor ability view in your own words.
2. In what way is a test for a general motor ability similar to an IQ test?
3. Henry termed his view the specificity of individual differences view. What did he mean by that?
4. Suppose you are asked to test a sample group of people for their general capacity to react quickly (i.e., reaction time ability). Suggest a methodology for assessing whether or not such an ability exists in your sample.

NOTES

- The association between two sets of ranks is just one type of correlation coefficient (often measured by a Spearman's Rho rank correlation coefficient), which is applied to ordinal types of data. The Pearson correlation coefficient is another type that is usually applied to data that are scaled, such as time and distance.
- Correlations (r values) between 0.0 and +1.0 are just half of the story. Correlation values can also range between 0.0 and −1.0. In ranked data, for example, a perfect negative correlation of $r = -1.0$ would occur if the first-ranked person on one test scored last on the second test, the second-ranked person on one test scored second to last on the second test, and so on. Negative correlations could occur for scaled data such as when a good score on one test and a good score on another test are in opposite directions because of the nature of the variable measured. An example would be time and distance: a good time score is as low as possible (such as for the 100-meter sprint), but a good distance score is as high as possible (such as for the long jump).

SUGGESTED READINGS

Cayleff, S.E. (1992). The "Texas Tomboy": The life and legend of Babe Didrikson Zaharias. *Organization of American Historians, 7*(1), 29-33. www.oah.org/pubs/magazine/sport/cayleff.html.

Henry, F.M. (1968). Specificity vs. generality in learning motor skill. In R.C. Brown & G.S. Kenyon (Eds.), *Classical studies on physical activity* (pp. 331-340). Englewood Cliffs, NJ: Prentice Hall. (Original work published in 1958.)

Hunt, P. (2000). 2. Babe Didrikson Zaharias, 1911-1956: Ultimate multisport athlete won three Olympic medals to go with 31 LPGA titles. http://sportsillustrated.cnn.com/siforwomen/top_100/2.

Park, R.J., Brooks, G.A., & Scott, M.K. (n.d.). In memoriam: Franklin M. Henry, Professor of Physical Education, Emeritus, UC Berkeley, 1909-1993. www.universityofcalifornia.edu/senate/inmemoriam/rranklinmhenry.html.

Schmidt, R.A., & Lee, T.D. (2011). Individual differences and capabilities. In *Motor control and learning: A behavioral emphasis* (5th ed., pp. 297-324). Champaign, IL: Human Kinetics.

LEARNING TO WIN FROM LOSING

Why is the learning–performance distinction important?

One day, Michelle Wie might be remembered as one of the greatest golfers of all time. At the age of 14 she was pounding out 300-yard (274 m) drives and not only competing in Ladies Professional (LPGA) Tour events, but also performing quite well in them. Her talent is undeniable. But controversy surrounded this exceptional athlete because of her desire to compete in PGA Tour events, which traditionally have included only male competitors. Wie has performed admirably in some of these events. For example, in the 2004 Sony Open, she shot rounds of 72 and 68 and missed the 36-hole cut by just a single stroke. Her two-round total of 140 placed her in a tie for 80th, which was better than 53 male professionals, including PGA stars Zach Johnson, Hunter Mahan, and Adam Scott. However, Wie has not performed well in most of the other PGA events she has entered, including a 139th-place finish (out of 141 players) at the 2007 Sony Open.

Many argued that Wie should stop competing in PGA Tour events and concentrate her efforts on the LPGA Tour. The typical argument was that her skill development as a golfer was being stalled by repeated failures in PGA Tour events, and that if she concentrated on LPGA events instead, the greater chance for success would escalate her skill development.

I argue that there is a fundamental flaw in this theory, because it falls into a trap known as the learning–performance distinction. The trap underlies one of the most misunderstood concepts in motor learning research, so let's start by defining the two terms. Motor skills researchers use the term *performance* to refer to a single observation. It could be a score or outcome that reflects the value of a single attempt at a motor skill, or perhaps an average score that statistically summarizes a number of attempts. An 18- or 36-hole score, or a final placement ranking in a tournament, might indicate a representative performance score in the case of a golfer. The term *learning* is used quite specifically to refer to a stable improvement in skill over time—an improvement that has specifically occurred as the result of practice. The problem illustrated by the criticisms leveled at Michelle Wie is that the critics fail to consider the difference between performance and learning; they mistakenly confuse her failures to improve her performance in men's PGA events as a failure to learn from these experiences. Let's use another example to illustrate this distinction between performance and learning.

Suppose you like to bowl, play regularly in a league, and also practice occasionally. Two years ago your average was 110, last year it was 120, and this year it is 130. Those averages probably indicate that you have become a better bowler as a result of learning: the scores indicate improvements that appear to be rather stable and that have resulted from practice.

So, does this mean that you will score a 130 the next time you bowl? Not necessarily, because there are many reasons for the fluctuations in scores that occur from game to game. Next time you may score well below your average because you are not feeling well, your shoes are too tight, or the crowd is very noisy that night. But this does not mean that you have suddenly lost some of your learned skill. You may score well above your average because you try extra hard to impress someone, or because everything just seems to be well focused (your mojo is working). As before, this does not mean that you have suddenly had a change in learned skill, because there is no indication that the sudden improvement in performance reflects a stable and permanent change in your capability to perform.

At any one time we have a theoretical capability for attaining a certain level of performance. When that theoretical capability changes to a higher level as a result of practice, we can say with confidence that we have learned. The confusion lies in the fact that individual performances may sometimes exceed or not live up to these theoretical capabilities. These fluctuations are expected and in no way diminish or detract from the performer's theoretical capability to perform at a certain skill level.

What I have described is the typical distinction between learning and performance. But, there is another side to this issue, the one that can be applied to Michelle Wie. The issue concerns the situation in which performances do not appear to change, or appear to be getting worse. Does that mean that learning is *not* occurring? Let's go back to the bowling example.

Suppose that this year your average was 120, which is the same as it was last year. You may take the absence of a stable improvement, despite all of your practice, as evidence that your learning has stalled. But, as it turns out, last year your league bowled Tuesday nights, which is your day off. This year you bowl on Wednesday nights, one hour after completing your 10-hour work shift. You are typically tired and hungry on league nights, and your bowling scores suffered this year as a result. What does all this suggest? What is your theoretical capability to bowl, and has this changed from last year, despite the change in your bowling night? Could it be that you actually *have* improved (i.e., learned), but the feeling of fatigue and other factors directly related to your work schedule prevented you from actually performing up to these expectations?

The point here is that making inferences about learning requires evidence that goes beyond a single performance or sometimes even a set of performances. Under what circumstances were these performances observed? Are there mitigating factors that might explain why the theoretical true score differs from the observed score? The absence of any observable change in performance does not mean that the unobservable (that theoretical capability to perform at a certain level of skill) has not improved.

Michelle Wie took a very different route in the development of her golfing skill. Her decision to compete in PGA events placed enormous pressures on her to perform, and only an exceptional result would have convinced the public that she was benefiting from these extreme challenges. All we could observe were her scores in these events. The unobservable, however, what she has learned by playing in these events, can never be truly understood. I suspect that if she achieves the rank of one of the greatest players of all time, it will be due in no small measure to these experiences competing against the very best golfers in the world.

SELF-DIRECTED LEARNING ACTIVITIES

1. In your own words, explain the distinction between performance and learning.
2. What is the difference between a theoretical true score and an observed score?
3. Suggest a reason a person's observed score might exceed the true score, and a reason the observed score might fail to achieve the level of the true score.
4. Identify another sport, athlete, or situation in which the failure to account for the learning–performance distinction has resulted in an inappropriate conclusion.

NOTES

- Babe Zaharias (see "The Babe") was the first woman to compete in a men's PGA event.
- Here is a sampling of some of the criticism of Michele Wie's decision to compete in PGA Tour events, from two sports commentary sites:

  www.tinyurl.com/wiecriticism1

  www.tinyurl.com/wiecriticism2
- Michelle Wie won her second LPGA Tour title in Winnipeg, Manitoba, at the 2010 CN Canadian Women's Open.

SUGGESTED READINGS

Schmidt, R.A. (1972). The case against learning and forgetting scores. *Journal of Motor Behavior, 4,* 79-88.

Schmidt, R.A., & Lee, T.D. (2011). Motor learning concepts and research methods. In *Motor control and learning: A behavioral emphasis* (5th ed., pp. 327-346). Champaign, IL: Human Kinetics.

What is the practical impact
of ineffective training methods?

In many structured learning situations, a preset, limited amount of time is available for practice. A high school gym teacher may devote two weeks to gymnastics skills. A college skills practicum may be one hour per day, three days per week, over a six-week period. A course in standard first aid training may take place over 16 hours on one weekend. In all of these examples, the task of the instructor (or someone who facilitates the learning process) is to maximize the amount learned in the limited amount of time that has been set aside for training. To do this, the instructor must carefully organize how the time is spent to achieve the most learning. So, how does one evaluate the relative effectiveness of training under these rigid time constraints?

A concept that is useful to consider in these situations is zero-sum training. The term comes from the concept of zero-sum games, such as chess. In the game of chess, each player begins with 16 pieces, and each player captures some of the other's pieces as the game progresses. A player cannot gain a piece without the other player losing a piece. The total number of pieces captured by one player will always equal the number of pieces that have been surrendered by the other player. In other words, the number of the pieces captured (+) plus the number surrendered (−) will always sum to zero.

The time spent in a specific activity becomes critically important in a time-limited skills training course for the same reason that chess is a zero-sum game. Comparing two methods of training, the less effective method has two disadvantages: (1) it is less productive than the other method in terms of its impact on learning, and (2) it uses up time that could have been spent engaged in the other, more effective method of training. Zero-sum training is simply the concept that every minute engaged in an ineffective method of practice is equal to a minute that could have been spent in a more effective method of practice. Quite simply, the ineffective method of practice is doubly ineffective because it wastes one hour of the learner's time, reducing by one hour the amount of time that could have been spent in more effective practice.

Those who accept the challenge of teaching any activity with limited time allocations for training should be aware of the zero-sum concept. As will be discussed in chapter 9, research suggests quite clearly that some training methods and strategies pay off in better learning than others do. According to the zero-sum concept, then, it is doubly important that facilitators ensure that their practice methods and techniques are as theoretically and practically sound as possible to establish an effective learning environment.

SELF-DIRECTED LEARNING ACTIVITIES

1. Explain the zero-sum training concept in your own words.
2. Explain why the zero-sum training concept is most appropriate for situations in which practice time is limited.
3. Why does the zero-sum training concept not apply to someone who has unlimited time to devote to training?

SUGGESTED READINGS

Schmidt, R.A., & Lee, T.D. (2011). Motor learning concepts and research methods. In *Motor control and learning: A behavioral emphasis* (5th ed., pp. 327-346). Champaign, IL: Human Kinetics.

Zero sum. (2010, October 5). In *Wikipedia.* Retrieved from http://en.wikipedia.org/wiki/zero-sum.

CHAPTER NINE

ORGANIZING PRACTICE

As mentioned in the story "Zero-Sum Training" in chapter 8, a poor practice regimen is doubly problematic when practice time is limited. In this chapter I discuss three issues in which time management, and hence practice efficiency and effectiveness, is directly affected by the way practice is conducted and augmented feedback is provided. The frequent lament of the average golfer ("But I Was Great on the Practice Range!") most likely results from poor practice strategies. Quite simply, the question is this: Why do people practice in a manner that is so unlike how they are required to play the game?

We live in a world that is drenched with information. The availability, immediacy, and richness of communication limit the need for self-generated information. In "The Coach as a Dictionary" and "The Golfer's Little Helper," I discuss what happens when the lines of communication are closed. The result is a paradoxical equation in which more becomes less and less becomes more.

But I Was Great on the Practice Range!

How does practice repetition influence performance and learning?

If you go to any golf driving range and watch people practice, you will quickly notice that most, if not all, people do at least two things: (1) they hit shot after shot after shot with the same club, and (2) after moving to the putting green, they putt ball after ball after ball from exactly the same spot. And yet, often these same golfers, when playing a round of golf, say in frustration as yet another ball goes into the water, or after another four-putt green, "I don't understand it; I was playing so well in practice yesterday."

The problem arises from misunderstanding the distinction between performance and learning (see "Learning to Win From Losing" in chapter 8) and how practice effectiveness and efficiency affect learning. The common view among many golfers is that you can "groove the swing" by making frequent repetitions in a short period of time. For example, let's say the practicing golfer takes out a 7 iron and hits the first ball poorly. A second ball is struck a little better, and by the sixth ball, our golfer is hitting the 7 iron much better. So, the golfer now hits another 10 or 15 balls in immediate succession, trying to "stamp in" a memory of those good shots. A similar fate occurs on the putting green. The first ball comes up short, the next is long, and the next is close but wide. The golfer continues to stroke putts from the same location until sinking one, and then continues to putt a few more to stamp in the memory of the swing that produced the putt that went into the hole.

What is wrong with this method of practice? Well, a number of things, actually. But the most fundamental problem is that learning does not occur by stamping in memories by rote repetition. The achievement of some objective, such as striking a golf ball, represents a motor problem, and the process of coordinating the activities of the central nervous system represents the solution to the problem. The acquisition of motor skills is a process of solving the problem in ways that become increasingly more reliable with practice.

In many respects, the process of motor learning is similar to the process involved in other types of learning, such as learning multiplication rules. Let's say, for example, that you were helping students learn longhand multiplication and posed the following problem for them to solve: $22 \times 17 = ?$. Immediately after they had solved the problem, would it be advisable to pose the same problem to them again? No, of course not. The reason is that they could (and would) come up with the solution to the problem (374) without going through the multiplication process. If your goal is to help your students learn the process of finding the solution, then immediately repeating the same problem would eliminate the requirement to go through the process of solving the problem again, because they could simply recall the answer. The effective teacher, therefore, uses a variety of questions that require the student to practice the process of longhand multiplication. But note that you could use the same question again later, after the students have forgotten the original solution to the problem. This example points out a very interesting conundrum: having a memory of the solution to the problem actually prevents or discourages us from carrying out the very activities we are trying to learn. We could phrase this another way by saying that forgetting has a beneficial effect on learning!

Motor skills researchers, starting with pioneers John Shea and Robyn Morgan, have addressed this issue of how to optimize the scheduling of practice using a variety of methods. In many of these studies, people are asked to learn several variations of a motor task and are given numerous practice attempts for each task. Two types of practice schedules are often compared: blocked practice and random practice. In blocked practice, the learners make all of their practice attempts for any one version of the motor task in immediate succession. This is a form of drill training, similar to the training of the golfer who hits all of his 7-iron shots in a row, then puts that club away for the remainder of the practice session. In random practice, the learner never practices the same task twice in a row (the golfer in our example would use a different club for each consecutive shot on the golf range). These two practice schedules are the same in terms of the amount of practice and the number of attempts made on each task; the only difference is the order in which the attempts are scheduled.

What is typically found in these types of studies is that blocked practice results in better performance than does random practice during the practice period itself. This is most likely due to the fact that random practice is much more demanding than blocked practice, and by its very nature is prone to less effective performance during the practice period (in the case of golf, while on the practice range). However, as in most studies of motor learning, one must keep in mind the distinction between factors that affect temporary changes in performance and those that have a more permanent influence on learning (see "Learning to Win From Losing" in chapter 8). In studies that measure the retention and transfer of the skills practiced, researchers have found that random practice results in better performance after the completion of practice—and hence, better learning—than blocked practice does.

Random practice might be more effective than blocked practice for several reasons. Some researchers have suggested that the demands of random practice add "desirable difficulty" that elevates the effort undertaken during practice. Of course, like most factors that increase the level of difficulty during practice, there will likely be a decrement in performance. The desirable part is that the learner will be better off in the long run because of the increased effort required to match the elevated difficulty of practice.

Another factor that is likely at work here concerns what is called the specificity of practice. Repeated performance of a single task is not typical of the way we perform most of the motor skills in our daily repertoires. To be sure, a golfer does not hit multiple shots in a row with the same club, or take multiple putts from the same distance, when playing a round of golf, just as LeBron James does not attempt 20 free throws in a row during a basketball game. So, why conduct practice in a manner that is so different from the conditions under which you are later required to perform? The take-home message of practice specificity is that we should anticipate the conditions to be confronted later, and then design the practice conditions to match them as closely as possible.

Every shot on the golf course poses a specific and unique problem for the golfer, who responds by trying to solve the problem with a specific and unique activity of the central nervous system. By repeatedly using the same club or putting from the same distance during practice sessions, many golfers run into the frustrating trap of trying to repeat solutions rather than solve problems. Golfers who practice effectively have discovered that solving problems in practice results in learning that helps them solve problems on the course.

In the end, choosing which practice schedule to use boils down to a cost–benefit analysis. The cost of random practice is a demanding practice routine, but the benefit is greater improvement in skill level. The golfer who complains about playing so well on the practice range was likely fooled into thinking that performance in blocked practice was a sign of good things to follow on the course. For this golfer, the cost–benefit analysis has worked in the opposite direction. The benefit of good performance on the practice range came at a cost of poor learning.

SELF-DIRECTED LEARNING ACTIVITIES

1. Define *blocked practice* and *random practice* in your own words.
2. How could you use the concept of specificity of practice to design a golf practice session?
3. Suppose a golfer were told that she could use only one ball when practicing putting. What benefit do you think this constraint might have on learning?
4. Design an experiment in which you compare skill improvements from blocked and random practice schedules, using any sport skill.

NOTES

- Larry Jacoby was one of the first researchers to discuss the conundrum of why forgetting benefits learning. Here are a couple of his articles:

    Jacoby, L.L. (1978). On interpreting the effects of repetition: Solving a problem versus remembering a solution. *Journal of Verbal Learning and Verbal Behavior, 17,* 649-667.

    Cuddy, L.J., & Jacoby, L.L. (1982). When forgetting helps memory. An analysis of repetition effects. *Journal of Verbal Learning and Verbal Behavior, 21,* 451-467.

- Many types of practice schedules other than random and blocked have been studied in research investigations. However, random and blocked schedules represent the extreme ends of the drilling versus nonrepetitive practice continuum.

- Robert Bjork, a psychologist and avid golfer at UCLA, coined the term *desirable difficulty.*

SUGGESTED READINGS

Lee, T.D., & Magill, R.A. (1983). The locus of contextual interference in motor-skill acquisition. *Journal of Experimental Psychology: Learning, Memory, and Cognition, 9,* 730-746.

Lee, T.D., & Simon, D.A. (2004). Contextual interference. In A.M. Williams & N.J. Hodges (Eds.), *Skill acquisition in sport: Research, theory and practice* (pp. 29-44). London: Routledge.

Schmidt, R.A., & Lee, T.D. (2011). Conditions of practice. In *Motor control and learning: A behavioral emphasis* (5th ed.). (pp. 347-392). Champaign, IL: Human Kinetics.

Shea, J.B., & Morgan, R.L. (1979). Contextual interference effects on the acquisition, retention, and transfer of a motor skill. *Journal of Experimental Psychology: Human Learning and Memory, 5,* 179-187.

THE COACH AS A DICTIONARY

What roles does augmented feedback play in motor learning?

When was the last time you looked up a word in a dictionary? What was the word you looked up? Why did you look it up? The last word I looked up was *exasperate*. I wanted to use it in a sentence that I was writing and needed to verify the exact meaning of the word and to make sure that my spelling was correct. As it turned out, I was correct about the meaning, but I had the spelling wrong. I don't tend to use a dictionary often, but it is always useful when I do. The dictionary provides me with gold standard information when the reliability of my own knowledge is in doubt.

A coach, instructor, or teacher who facilitates the motor learning process is very much like a dictionary. This person provides the learner with reliable information, usually about something the learner is doing incorrectly and often about something the learner is unaware that she is doing incorrectly.

Often, our awareness of the accuracy of our intended actions arises from sensory mechanisms within the body. Our eyes provide visual information; our ears provide auditory information; our skin provides tactile information; and sensory mechanisms in the muscles and joints provide information about movement, called proprioceptive (or sometimes kinesthetic) information. Researchers call this information *inherent feedback* because it arises from within the person and is "fed back" to the brain to update the current status of either an ongoing movement or one that has just been completed (see "The Curling Draw" in chapter 7 for more on the closed-loop process of using feedback to regulate movement).

People who facilitate the learning process represent another source of information about the status of our actions. For example, they can describe something verbally, such as informing a diver that her tuck was opening too soon during the spin. They can also provide us with visual information, such as a video of the just-completed dive. Researchers use the term *augmented feedback* to describe this type of input because the information does not arise inherently from our own senses; rather, an external source has fed back additional, augmented information that supplements the inherent information we have received from our senses.

For many years learning theory was dominated by the view that augmented feedback is an essential part of the skill acquisition process. Many believed that learning would be enhanced when inherent feedback was supplemented by augmented feedback (1) as often as possible, (2) as soon as possible after the completion of the performance, (3) with as much information as possible, and (4) generally, in any other way that would help the learner make the greatest amount of improvement as fast as possible. Those theoretical views were supported by data from a large number of experiments.

However, a research team led by Richard Schmidt discovered a glitch in these findings. The researchers found that many of the positive effects of augmented feedback were restricted to the trials during which frequent and immediate augmented feedback was provided. If learners were subsequently left to perform the task only with their sources of inherent feedback, then performance suffered in many situations. Moreover, performance when the augmented feedback was removed suffered more so than it did in situations in which augmented feedback had been provided sparingly during practice, or delayed for a period of time during which the learners were asked to interpret their own inherent feedback. Of course, this is yet another example of the important distinction between performance and learning (see "Learning to Win From Losing" in chapter 8 and "But I Was Great on the Practice Range!" earlier in this chapter).

Researchers now agree that augmented feedback can be an excellent supplement to the learning environment if provided in ways that challenge learners to better understand their own sources of inherent feedback. But, when it is provided too often, or too soon, or in such a way that it is used as a substitute for understanding the status of inherent feedback, then the learner can be affected in a negative way. Some suggest that learners come to rely on augmented feedback as a crutch to support performance, and are unable to sustain that level of performance when the crutch is removed.

A good example of augmented feedback occurs in baseball. A pitcher can sometimes run into control problems during a game when he repeatedly makes an unintentional biomechanical error. The result is that he temporarily forgets how to throw the ball to a specific location. A good pitching coach can spot the problem and help the pitcher correct it. However, according to the rules of baseball, the coach can confer with the pitcher only once during play; a second conference results in the pitcher's removal from the game. Therefore, it is to the pitcher's advantage to learn how and why he makes errors that result in certain outcomes, but more important, to understand what his inherent feedback means, so he can detect and correct his mistakes without the coach's augmented feedback.

When should augmented feedback be provided, and when should it be withheld? One way to think about optimizing the provision of augmented feedback is to think again in terms of the dictionary analogy discussed earlier, which provides gold standard feedback to the learner. We do not consult a dictionary for every word we write. Instead, we count on the reliability of our internal spell-checker to know when we have made an error.

Only when we question the reliability of our internal spell-checker should we consult a dictionary. In terms of learning motor skills, to be independent, we must learn to understand what our bodies tell us. To do that, we need to learn to interpret inherent feedback, and supplement it with augmented feedback only when necessary, as with the dictionary. The reliability of our own spell-checker is optimized when we no longer need a dictionary at all. Independence from reliance on augmented feedback is another marker of motor skill expertise.

SELF-DIRECTED LEARNING ACTIVITIES

1. Define *augmented feedback* in your own words.
2. Give an example of the difference between augmented feedback and inherent feedback in driving a car with a manual transmission.
3. A coach who tells a learner about a movement error is providing one specific type of augmented feedback (verbal). Using a video camera to provide feedback is another method. List three other qualitatively different ways of delivering augmented feedback.
4. Describe an experimental methodology that contrasts the benefits of various frequencies of augmented feedback.

NOTES

- I find that an online dictionary is very helpful and handy when writing

  www.merriam-webster.com

- Many of the research glitches that led to the mistaken conclusion that more augmented feedback was always better were reported in two important papers by Schmidt's research team:

  Salmoni, A.W., Schmidt, R.A., & Walter, C.B. (1984). Knowledge of results and motor learning: A review and critical reappraisal. *Psychological Bulletin, 95,* 355-386.

  Schmidt, R.A., & Bjork, R.A. (1992). New conceptualizations of practice: Common principles in three paradigms suggest new concepts for training. *Psychological Science, 3,* 207-217.

SUGGESTED READINGS

Schmidt, R.A., & Lee, T.D. (2011). Augmented feedback. In *Motor control and learning: A behavioral emphasis* (5th ed., pp. 393-428). Champaign, IL: Human Kinetics.

What elements of motor learning are neglected when we use mechanical training aids?

There is a TV channel devoted solely to golf. I'm not kidding. Golf tournaments, highlight shows, and instructional lessons are the main shows on the Golf Channel. Squeezed between these shows are half-hour-long infomercials for various products. Most of them drive me crazy.

The most annoying of these infomercials advertise practice aids—guidance devices specifically designed to constrain the arms, legs, hands, head, or other body parts so that the person's motions are more or less forced to conform to a certain path. These practice aids come in many forms. Some put physical restrictions on your movements—for example, by having you move the club along a string or length of plastic that constrains the motion of the golf club along some "ideal" swing path. Some aids project a beam of light that shows you the alignment of the club relative to the target. Others physically constrain the distance between the hands or arms so that a constant relationship is maintained throughout the swing. The number and variety of practice aids on the market are staggering. But don't take my word for it. Search on the phrases *golf practice aids* or *golf training aids* in your Internet browser and see what comes up.

To get an idea of how effective (or ineffective) these practice aids might be, I want you to try a little experiment. The intention here is to simulate what a golf practice aid actually does when you use it. You will need a blank sheet of paper, a piece of cardboard, a pencil, a ruler, and a pair of scissors or a utility knife. First, draw a line on the piece of cardboard that is exactly 4 inches (10 cm) in length. Then, using the scissors or knife, cut a small 4-inch-long trough out of the cardboard. The trough only needs to be wide enough to insert a pencil. Place the sheet of paper on a table and, using a pencil in the cardboard trough, draw a 4-inch line using a quick left-to-right movement on the paper. Then draw another 4-inch line. Do this eight more times. According to the logic of golf practice aids, you have just learned to make a perfect 4-inch line by making 10 flawless repetitions of your movement goal. Now, put everything away.

About an hour later, get out another blank sheet and draw 10 more 4-inch lines, but don't look at the lines you drew earlier. And this time, draw the 4-inch lines using a straightedge that does not have any markings on it that might clue you in on what length to draw the line. This is a test to see how well you have remembered what you learned earlier. After you have drawn all 10 lines, measure the length of each line and compute the mean of the 10 new lines (see "Cutting Wood and Missing Putts" in chapter 4). Compare the mean of the lines that you just drew in this retention test to the perfect mean of 4 inches that you made during the guided trials. If you are similar to most people, the average line length is likely to be either longer or shorter than the mean of the cardboard-guided trials. And if you are like some people, that average is *considerably* different from the lines you drew in guided trials.

Drawing lines is a simple task, of course, and bears no resemblance at all to the golf swing or most of the complex actions we make in everyday activities. However, the principles involved in learning are similar. The goal of most guidance aids, especially those in golf, is to prevent the introduction of, or drastically restrict the possibility of introducing, error into the movement. Once error is eliminated, the idea (or theory) is that the person can then make many repetitions of the correct movement and, in so doing, "groove" that learned representation into the central nervous system. This idea is based on the same logic that I discussed earlier ("But I Was Great on the Practice Range!") and is consistent with earlier theories of learning that stated that making errors resulted in learning to make errors. The logic was that, to combat the problem of learning to make errors, an activity or aid that helped someone make correct movements could be used to promote the learning of correct movements.

But that is *not* how humans learn motor skills. Based on a wealth of accumulated research in the past half-century, human motor learning theorists believe that what happens is almost the opposite: we learn from making all types of actions, both correct and incorrect. There are three key steps in the learning process: (1) make a movement plan prior to action, (2) execute the action, and then (3) evaluate the movement in relation to the original plan. The logic that underlies most guidance devices is that step 2 is the only important one. But, in fact, steps 1 and 3 are equally important, if not more so; they help us clarify what we are trying to achieve with the movement and evaluate it later using both inherent and augmented feedback (see "The Coach as a Dictionary").

The overuse of most golf practice aids undermines both of these two key information steps for learning. First, a guidance device discourages advance movement planning because a correct movement can be achieved by simply following the guide. Second, because no movement plan was devised in advance, there is no referent against which to compare the outcome after the movement has been completed. Moreover, because errors are virtually eliminated, there is little need for evaluation anyway. A guidance device will not create an effective learning process regardless of how many repetitions are made. In fact, it is likely to be detrimental to learning because every minute you spend using the device is a minute you did not spend engaged in more effective practice (see "Zero-Sum Training" in chapter 8).

Some of these infomercials suggest that using their products will guarantee lower golf scores. Sadly, repetitive use of these practice aids simply cannot be effective, no matter what the infomercial tells you. And this advice comes to you without the three easy payments of $29.95.

SELF-DIRECTED LEARNING ACTIVITIES

1. Define *guidance*, in terms of motor learning, in your own words.

2. Conduct the experiment described in the story using two friends who do not anticipate the purpose of your experiment. Calculate their constant error (CE) and variable error (VE) scores (see "Cutting Wood and Missing Putts" in chapter 4). Now run the experiment again with two other friends, but this time, alternate guided and nonguided practice trials (five each). Compare the retention test CE and VE scores of the first two friends with those of the latter two.

3. Find a golf guidance device (or a guidance device used in another sport) on the Internet and critically analyze the manufacturer's claims about its effectiveness for motor learning.

4. Design a research investigation in which you assess the effectiveness of the golf guidance device you identified in question 3. What are the appropriate control, or experimental, conditions against which you are comparing the golf guidance device, and why did you choose these particular comparison conditions?

NOTES

• The following research study shows a typical finding of the detrimental effect of relying on a guidance aid for motor learning. The article also provides many useful references to earlier research.

   Sidaway, B., Ahn, S., Boldeau, P., Griffin, S., Noyes, B., & Pelletier, K. (2008). A comparison of manual guidance and knowledge of results in the learning of a weight-bearing skill. *Journal of Neurologic Physical Therapy, 32,* 32-38.

SUGGESTED READINGS

Marchal Crespo, L., & Reinkensmeyer, D.J. (2008). Haptic guidance can enhance motor learning of a steering task. *Journal of Motor Behavior, 40,* 545-556.

Schmidt, R.A., & Lee, T.D. (2011). Augmented feedback. In *Motor control and learning: A behavioral emphasis* (5th ed., pp. 393-428). Champaign, IL: Human Kinetics.

CHAPTER TEN

SKILL DEVELOPMENT

In chapter 9 I discussed several ways practice and feedback could be structured and the resulting impact on learning that would likely occur. The stories in this chapter focus more specifically on the process of skill development—what is learned and the process by which that learning occurs. Although learning by means of observation (or modeling) is a powerful "off-site" practice tool, in "Bend It Like Becker" you might be surprised to find out who makes the best model. W.C. Fields makes a surprise reappearance on the Internet in "Sport Snake Oils." There is something that may surprise you about your cell phone and your computer in "The Keypad," although you could probably continue to use both very well without reading this story. And no hockey fan would doubt that Wayne Gretzky was one of the best who ever laced up a pair of skates. But the underlying reasons for his superior talent may surprise you.

What types of models are best to observe when learning a skill?

Yeah, I know—you think this is a typo. After all, David Beckham was one of the best soccer players in the world for a while, or at least one of the most recognizable. And his name was popularized in the title of the movie *Bend It Like Beckham*. My argument here, however, is that you might just learn more if you tried to bend it like Becker (our fictional, unskilled soccer player) rather than Beckham. This story concerns the issue of observational learning and what we gain by watching a model.

Athletes who practice to develop sport skills would love to have the skills of professional athletes. Therefore, it is not surprising that most instructors and coaches of sport skills believe that professional athletes serve as the best models for demonstrating sport skills. For example, conventional wisdom would suggest that to hit a better tennis backhand, we should watch people like Serena Williams or Roger Federer. To learn to throw a nasty slider, we need to study Roy Halladay or John Smoltz. So, to learn to hook a penalty kick around a line of defenders, isn't the best idea simply to watch Beckham bend it?

Well, maybe yes and maybe no. There are a few assumptions to be made about the process of learning by watching the actions of a model. Some of these assumptions, but not all of them, would appear to favor the use of a professional athlete as a model. In their favor, the most highly skilled athletes usually possess the best skills to perform their particular sports. So it would seem natural that to become a better performer, one would need to watch someone who performs those skills at their highest level. So, one question would be this: How well can we perceive skills just by watching? Or perhaps a more fundamental question is What do we perceive when we see people move?

A clever research method introduced some years ago by Gunnar Johansson revealed that people were able to observe quite fine details simply by watching other people move. In his original study, Johansson filmed actors dressed in black body suits against a black background. Johansson attached reflective markers to strategic body parts (mostly joints) so that after editing, someone watching the film could not see the outlines of the people themselves. Instead, all they could see was the motions of the reflective markers as the person wearing the body suit moved about in the environment. Johansson (and others who have used similar methods) found that their research participants could readily identify a number of features from the motions of the people on the video. For example, they could distinguish males from females, recognize friends, and even identify different types of animals from their gaits.

More recently, researchers have shown that various actions are identifiable, too, just from watching the motions of these white dots. Actions such as kicking a soccer ball, throwing a ball, and jumping were all readily perceived just from the movement of white dots on a video screen. These experiments demonstrate quite conclusively that humans have the capability to perceive fine details of temporal and spatial activities, even when provided quite restricted visual information.

Clearly, we must be good at picking up much more information from watching full videos rather than just watching moving dots. So, the answer to my earlier question is yes, we can perceive motor skills just by watching. However, does watching a professional athlete perform skills provide the optimal opportunity to learn? This is a difficult question to answer, because it presupposes that the average observer knows what to look *at* and what to look *for*. But that is not necessarily so. The research on this question suggests that skilled athletes serve as the best models for those who already possess some skill in the activity. Learning is facilitated even more if an instructor can help the observer attend to specific features displayed by the model.

But, another research area suggests that watching completely unskilled models can be a useful learning tool as well. This is especially true if, for example, the model is a member of a beginner-level skills class and the instructor has asked that person to demonstrate some activity to the rest of the class. In this situation, the instructor can point out specific faults to both the model and those who are observing the model. The unskilled model demonstrates something that might be wrong, and the observers get to see what the model has performed. Most important, the observers also receive the augmented feedback provided by the instructor about the error that was made, and then are engaged in watching the model attempt to correct the error. This is a powerful observational learning situation because it engages the observer in the problem-solving process that captures the trial-and-error activities of the learner.

So, should we watch Beckham or Becker bend it? The conventional wisdom would suggest Beckham. From a motor learning perspective, however, there may be as much or more benefit from watching the unskilled Becker as there is from watching the very skilled Beckham, especially if the observers are novice learners.

SELF-DIRECTED LEARNING ACTIVITIES

1. Define the term *observational learning* in your own words.
2. Identify a skill that would be difficult to model effectively, and one that would be easy to model. What is it about these skills that makes them easy or difficult to model?

3. The story considers model skill as an important characteristic in the observational learning process. Identify four other model characteristics that could have an impact on observational learning.

4. Identify a research methodology you could use to assess the impact of one of the model characteristics that you identified in question 3.

NOTES

- The following websites have examples of point-light displays of biological motion:

  www.tinyurl.com/pointlight1

  www.tinyurl.com/pointlight2

  www.tinyurl.com/pointlight3

- Some very interesting observational learning research was conducted using point-light display techniques to model soccer skills, including this one:

  Horn, R.R., Scott, M.A., Williams, A.M., & Hodges, N.J. (2005). Visual search and coordination changes in response to video and point-light demonstrations without KR. *Journal of Motor Behavior, 37,* 265-274.

SUGGESTED READINGS

Hodges, N.J., & Franks, I.M. (2002). Modelling coaching practice: The role of instruction and demonstration. *Journal of Sports Sciences, 20,* 793-811.

Janelle, C.M., Champenoy, J.D., Coombes, S.A., & Mousseau, M.B. (2003). Mechanisms of attentional cueing during observational learning to facilitate skill acquisition. *Journal of Sports Sciences, 21,* 825-838.

Johansson, G. (1973). Visual perception of biological motion and a model for its analysis. *Perception & Psychophysics, 14,* 201-211.

McCullagh, P., & Weiss, M.R. (2001). Modeling: Considerations for motor skill performance and psychological responses. In R.N. Singer, H.A. Hausenblas, & C.M. Janelle (Eds.), *Handbook of sport psychology* (2nd ed., pp. 205-238). New York: Wiley.

Schmidt, R.A., & Lee, T.D. (2011). Conditions of practice. In *Motor control and learning: A behavioral emphasis* (5th ed., pp. 347-392). Champaign, IL: Human Kinetics.

SPORT SNAKE OILS

Can visual training programs improve sport performance?

They come into town, peddle their wares, and then get out before their "snake oils" are discovered to be bogus. They claim that their elixirs will cure cancers, gout, heart problems, venereal diseases, and anything else that ails you. But, in fact, the only proven effect of these wares is that they make the snake oil sellers richer. The great comic actor W.C. Fields played a memorable one in the 1936 movie *Poppy*. The snake oil sellers of today don't pull into town. Rather, they appear on Internet sites peddling wares such as sport vision training programs. But their only proven effect is the same—the wares benefit only the sellers.

Don't get me wrong—vision is critically important for success in many sports. For example, drastic improvements in sport performance could be expected from programs that correct structural issues resulting in acuity problems and other visual deficits. However, these vision programs begin to turn into snake oil when they claim to be able to train the person to see better. The idea is actually pretty simple and sounds encouraging to people who are unfamiliar with the research in this area. If one could improve peripheral vision, object tracking, eye–hand coordination, depth perception, and other visual abilities that are important in many sports, then it would certainly be expected that improvements in sport performance would result.

Here is a visual training test comparable to those found on some Internet sites. The display in figure 10.1 is shown on the screen for about two seconds. After the display disappears, your task is to respond as quickly as possible by pressing the keys on your keyboard that match the arrows in the display.

The instructions are unclear at first, which I have a feeling was done deliberately to give the user a feeling of mastery after figuring them out

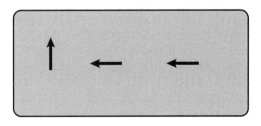

Figure 10.1 Sample A of a visual skills Internet trainer. This display is presented for about two seconds, after which the task is to type the arrow keys in the order displayed (right arrow, up arrow, down arrow key).

through trial and error. But in the end, it is a pretty easy task to perform. For this test, the correct response is to press the right, up, and down arrow keys in immediate succession as fast as possible. After you get a perfect trial, the site then takes you to the screen shown in figure 10.2, which, instead of being displayed for two seconds, is displayed for about one quarter of a second.

Your certain failure in the test in figure 10.2 prompts the website to tell you that although you were unsuccessful in performing the task this time, following completion of the training program you will have a much better chance of being successful. Similar programs are included that will help you train your tracking abilities and something called visual flexibility. There is no indication about how the training program will make you better at the task. Indeed, there is no indication about why or how the program will make you better at anything. Nevertheless, the implications are obvious, and the website lists numerous high school, university, national, and professional teams involved in a variety of sports as previous users of the product.

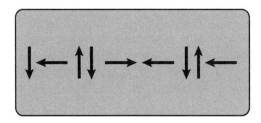

Figure 10.2 Sample B of a visual skills Internet trainer. This display is presented for about one quarter of a second, after which the near-impossible task is to remember and type the arrow keys in the order displayed.

Visual training programs like the one just described have been around for many years and earn their developers piles of money. But do they work? Bruce Abernethy and Joanne Wood, researchers at the University of Queensland in Australia, studied one of these programs using a prolonged intervention, which should have resulted in improved performance if the program had any value. If the benefit of visual training was generalizable to sport skills, which is one of the most important revenue-generating claims of these programs, their study should have showed improved performance following the program. They found that those in the training group did indeed improve their performance, but *only* on the tests of the vision program itself.

We know from over a century of research in motor learning that practice will improve performance in just about any type of task, so Abernethy and Wood's results support this general finding. Most important, though, the researchers found that the motor skills of those who had participated in the vision training program were no better than those of the control group. This finding is also no great surprise, because years of research in motor learning have taught us a lesson in this regard: Vision is important for providing the brain with information, but to use that information to benefit motor skill performance requires that we practice the specific processes that underlie performance. As discussed later in this chapter, Wayne Gretzky did not become one of the best hockey players of all time by training his visual system, but rather by training the anticipatory and perceptual processes that use vision as information input (see "Wayne Gretzky").

One further issue deserves comment regarding the Abernethy and Wood research. Suppose the participants in the training group had spent the same amount of time engaged in practice of the skills for their sport instead of participating in the general vision skills program. My guess is that their sport-specific skills would have had a much better chance for improvement than any benefit from the vision-training program. According to this view, these vision-training programs are actually detrimental to learning because they reduce the time that could have been spent in a more effective type of practice (see the rationale in "Zero-Sum Training" in chapter 8). By this view, the vision-training program did not enhance the development of sport-specific skills. It prevented learning.

The snake oil sellers of years gone by would plant an accomplice in the crowd of people gathered around. The task of the accomplice was to claim that the snake oil had worked, thereby lending more credence to the pitch and prompting a flurry of sales. The accomplice was not trained in medicine, had no scientific background, and was no doubt paid to say those things. Next time you see one of these vision training websites and listen to the claims and anecdotes of the athletes who swear that the product worked for them, ask yourself, *So what does modern-day snake oil taste like?*

SELF-DIRECTED LEARNING ACTIVITIES

1. Define *vision training* in your own words.
2. How does the concept of zero-sum training specifically apply to the evaluation of sport vision training programs?
3. Find a sport vision training program on the Internet and summarize the specific benefits the program promises. Is an accomplice listed?
4. How might you conduct a research investigation to evaluate the merits of the vision training program that you discovered in researching question 3?

NOTES

- A sample of W.C. Fields in *Poppy*:
  www.tinyurl.com/fieldspoppy

SUGGESTED READINGS

Abernethy, B., & Wood, J.M. (2001). Do generalized visual training programmes for sport really work? An experimental investigation. *Journal of Sports Sciences, 19,* 203-222.

Schmidt, R.A., & Lee, T.D. (2011). Retention and transfer. In *Motor control and learning: A behavioral emphasis* (5th ed., pp. 461-490). Champaign, IL: Human Kinetics.

How do explicit and implicit memories influence skilled performance?

Do the following thought experiment without looking at your cell phone. Imagine that you are calling the phone number of a close friend. Visually imagine your fingers as you press each of the numbers on your keypad. Now, use those same numbers that you imagined dialing on your cell phone and visually imagine yourself typing them on a calculator or the numeric keypad on a computer keyboard. Did you happen to notice anything different about how you imagined pressing those numbers in the two situations? You should have noticed a rather dramatic difference. If you didn't, then take a look at figure 10.3.

The layouts of the keypads on the cell phone and the calculator are not only different; in fact, they are the reverse of each other. When I point this

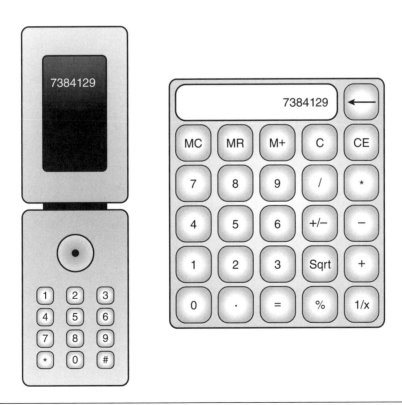

Figure 10.3 Do you notice a difference between the layout of a cell phone keypad and that of a calculator keypad?

out to students in my undergraduate classes, many are quite surprised. And yet, they are all quite proficient at using both cell phones and calculators and fluidly move back and forth between the two. So what does this suggest about how we can perform so skillfully without knowing some, fundamental features of the devices we are using? What does it say about the nature of perceptual and motor skill representation in memory in general?

One clue to an answer to these questions concerns the distinction between what researchers call explicit and implicit memory. In general, researchers use the term *explicit* to refer to features, concepts, relationships, and the like, about which you have a specific awareness that quite often you can verbalize. For example, you know the color of your bicycle and cell phone, and you may have a vivid memory of the last bike ride you took or the last phone conversation you had. These are called explicit memories because they can be recalled in rather detailed words and descriptions.

In contrast, the term *implicit* reflects a more loosely defined concept that refers to (mostly) nonverbalizable features of our actions. Implicit memories influence how we interact with the environment in ways about which we are not consciously aware, but which nevertheless influence our daily activities. Although you may recall the last phone number you dialed, you probably do not remember much about how you dialed the number or held the phone. You may recall the route you took on your last bike ride, but you likely don't remember much about the specific accelerations you applied to the bike at certain times, or the postural adjustments you made to go around corners. These implicit memories enable you to dial a phone number or lean into a curve while riding a bicycle, but often do not rise to any specific state of awareness. And yet, if it were not for these implicit memories, you would never be successful in placing a phone call or going for a ride on your bike.

In very general terms, explicit memories allow us to remember facts and details, and implicit memories enable us to do things.

The study of explicit and implicit memory suggests important features about how our brains are organized. Daniel Schacter, a neuropsychologist at Harvard University, reported a very interesting study about an amnesic patient with whom he played several rounds of golf. The patient displayed all the signs of a good implicit memory: his golfing skill was no worse than before he developed amnesia, and he displayed various behaviors on the course that were appropriate for the game of golf. In other words, he had no problem with the task of *how* to play the game. The problems that the patient encountered were associated with remembering the *what* of the game. He often forgot how many shots he had taken to complete a hole; he frequently forgot where his previous shot had landed; and on several occasions, after first hitting his ball and then waiting for Schacter to tee off, he started to tee his ball again because he had not remembered previously hitting his tee shot. The patient's amnesia seemed to be a specific impairment of explicit memory that left implicit memory relatively unaffected.

Unless you are told that the calculator and cell phone keypads are opposite in their layouts, you probably have no explicit memory of their difference. And yet you have been able to not only use them, but go back and forth between the two layouts with no apparent difficulty. The absence of an explicit memory that the two keypads are different appears to have no influence at all on the implicit memory involved in using them.

SELF-DIRECTED LEARNING ACTIVITIES

1. Define *explicit memory* and *implicit memory* in your own words.
2. Pick an activity of daily life, or a sporting activity, and provide examples of how explicit and implicit memory are used in the activity.
3. The terms *explicit* and *implicit* are sometimes interchanged with other terms in the literature (with only subtle differences in the distinction). Look up another memory dissociation scheme and briefly describe how if differs from the explicit–implicit distinction.
4. Describe a research methodology that you could use to assess whether or not the uses of a cell phone and a calculator are influenced by the specific awareness of their layout differences. Describe specifically how you would measure awareness and the nature of your performance measure.

NOTES

- Explicit memory = what, implicit memory = how, and intentions = why.
- Some friends with whom I regularly play golf also have trouble remembering how many shots they had taken on a previous hole; in their case, however, I seriously doubt that amnesia is the cause.

SUGGESTED READINGS

Schacter, D.L. (1983). Amnesia observed: Remembering and forgetting in a natural environment. *Journal of Abnormal Psychology, 92,* 236-242.

What role does skilled perception play in sport performance?

Although generally acknowledged as one of the greatest hockey players of all time, Wayne Gretzky was considered a mere mortal in terms of many hockey skills, such as skating, shooting, and stick handling. What many people believe set Gretzky apart from other professionals was his uncanny ability to read a play as it was developing—to know not only where each of his own teammates and the players of the other team were on the ice at any one time but to be able to predict where they would be in the future.

The ability to gather, process, and understand a large amount of information in a very short period of time is commonly referred to as skilled perception, and many believe that Wayne Gretzky was one of the best ever at doing that in hockey. Instead of seeing individual players on the ice, Gretzky probably saw, and could predict, the formation, dissolution, and reformation of patterns—spatial and temporal relationships among the players, the officials, and the dimensions of the playing surface.

Gretzky's ability to understand a vast amount of information in a very brief period of time is not peculiar to hockey players. Highly skilled perception is a requirement in many team sports, such as when a defensive middle linebacker in North American football must read an offensive play. The very best linebackers see the movements of the players on the field not as individuals but rather as components of a larger puzzle that is set in motion. They perceive pattern flows of information.

Research that provides clues about how Gretzky and other athletes use their exceptional perceptual skills was developed from a rather unlikely origin: the study of people who play the game of chess! Consider this experiment: You are sitting in front of a table on which a partially played game of chess sits beneath a cover. You cannot see the chess pieces until the experimenter uncovers the board, at which time you are given five seconds to study the layout and positioning of the pieces. After five seconds, the board is covered again and you are asked to re-create the board using a second chess set. How do you think you would do?

Unless you are an expert chess player (a chess master), your results would probably be similar to those found by DeGroot and, later, by Chase and Simon. You would probably remember some of the pieces and their locations on the board, but certainly not all of them. But if, in fact, you actually were a chess master, your performance would be quite different; you would probably remember most if not all of the pieces and their locations on the board. Because chess has logic, structure, and rules, the dynamics of game play take on patterns that have a certain predictability, if not similarity and familiarity, to the chess master. Remembering the layout of a partially played chess board after a brief glimpse is not so much a task of recalling the individual pieces. Rather, recall is more a task of remembering the patterns of or relationships among the pieces and perhaps being able to re-create how the play must have evolved for the pieces to be where they are at that point in the game.

But these researchers took their work one important step further. Let's say that you were to do the experiment again and see the board with the same number of pieces for another five seconds. This time, however, the pieces on the board do not represent the middle of a game, but rather, are randomly dispersed around the board, with no obvious gamelike structure to them. Because you are remembering the individual pieces and their locations, you can probably re-create the board as well as before. In the absence of a recognizable pattern to the array, however, the chess master is at a loss to understand the relationships among the individual pieces. The master will be forced to process each piece individually, rather than as part of a collective pattern, and his re-creation of this random board will likely be no better than yours.

It is not a big stretch to consider how chess, hockey, and football might have a common basis in terms of perception. All contain multiple players who change positions over a restricted playing area according to logic, structure, and rules that are specific to the game. Only the most highly skilled in their game, such as Wayne Gretzky, have developed the capability to understand the intricate dynamics of game flow and can do so in very brief periods of time with amazing precision. For Gretzky, being highly skilled at the motor components of hockey likely represented only a small part of his amazing talent.

SELF-DIRECTED LEARNING ACTIVITIES

1. Define *skilled perception* in your own words.
2. Pick another sport (other than hockey or American football) and describe the perceptual attributes that are required to attain a very high level of playing skill.
3. Describe the nature of perceptual expertise required to become skilled in the performance of a video game. How is the nature of this type of perceptual skill similar to or different from the sport skill that you described in question 2?
4. Find two people, one who is skilled at the game of chess and one who is not (but who is familiar with the game), and replicate the basic conditions of the Chase and Simon study. How do your results compare with theirs?

NOTES

- The play of Gretzky and some musings about his skills were captured nicely in Peter Gzowski's book:

    Gzowski, P. (1981). *The game of our lives.* Toronto: McClellan & Stewart.

SUGGESTED READINGS

Chase, W.G., & Simon, H.A. (1973). Perception in chess. *Cognitive Psychology, 4,* 55-81.

DeGroot, A.D. (1946). *Thought and choice in chess.* The Hague: Mouton.

Schmidt, R.A., & Lee, T.D. (2011). Human information processing. In *Motor control and learning: A behavioral emphasis* (5th ed., pp. 57-96). Champaign, IL: Human Kinetics.

Starkes, J.L., & Ericsson, K.A. (2003). (Eds.). *Expert performance in sport: Advances in research on sport expertise.* Champaign, IL: Human Kinetics.

Skill Retention

We perform skills every day without paying them much attention. Each morning I get on my bike and just assume that I have retained my riding skills. We take for granted that the driver of the bus we are riding, who is just returning from vacation, has not lost her driving skills. And we definitely hope that the doctor who performs delicate surgery has excellent retention of those skills since his last operation. But there is good reason to suspect that some assumptions are not well founded. "Shooting Two From the Line" suggests that there could well be a brief period of time at the start of performing these skills in which a loss of proficiency would be expected. But skill retention is a complex subject. "Like Riding a Bicycle" suggests that some aspects of skill are retained rather flawlessly over very long periods of time, whereas other memory attributes are lost very quickly. And the life story of Henry Gustav Molaison, known by many as H.M., provides a remarkable lesson in brain function and memory formation.

SHOOTING TWO FROM THE LINE

How does the warm-up decrement affect repeated performances?

Pay close attention to skilled carpenters as they hammer nails. They are remarkably efficient in their actions. Two or three strikes are usually all it takes to pound a long nail into a piece of wood. And, unlike me, skilled carpenters never miss hitting the nail on the head. Or, at least, they seldom do. The famous American psychologist E.L. Thorndike once observed that the only miss he ever observed a carpenter make came on the very first strike after a coffee break. Mere coincidence? Perhaps not.

The game of basketball provides another good example of the same phenomenon. The free throw in basketball represents a situation in which a player must perform a specific shot after a varying length of time since the last attempt. When fouled in the act of shooting, a player is awarded two consecutive foul shots. Is the second shot more likely to be successful than the first? In the mid-1980s, a research team investigated the Boston Celtics' shooting performance over the course of two NBA seasons. One of the many interesting findings of that investigation (see also "The Hot Hand" in chapter 4) concerned the success in shooting two free throws. The researchers found that the Celtics' players were successful on 70.6 percent of the first of the two free throw attempts, but they achieved success on 75.2 percent of the second of two consecutive free throw attempts—a level of success that was almost 5 percent higher than that of the first attempt. Why was there such a difference?

Motor skills researchers have studied a phenomenon that might explain the nail hammering and free throw observations and gave it a very simple and explanatory name: warm-up decrement. The idea is simple: When you take a break from performing a task, there is a temporary loss in the readiness to perform at your maximum potential. This doesn't occur, for example, when you are continually pounding nails because you remain focused and prepared for each action (although mental and physical fatigue may come into effect after long periods of work). But, after a break, there is a temporary loss of the abilities needed for performing at peak mental functioning, such as focus of attention, concentration, motor programming, and a combination of other cognitive factors that support performance. In basketball, a game that is in near-constant flow, the free throw is a unique situation in which the rules dictate that the game stand still momentarily. In stepping up to the free throw line, the player may be warmed up in a physiological sense, but perhaps not in the psychological sense of being maximally prepared to take the first of the two shots.

In his excellent review of the research on warm-up decrement, Jack Adams used the term *set* to refer to the psychological factors that support performance. In his view, warm-up decrement occurs because those psychological factors are not optimized when the athlete begins to initiate performance. In other words, there has been a loss of set.

One of the key goals of research on warm-up decrement has been to examine activities that might reinstate the appropriate set after a period of time has elapsed since the last performance attempt. The research suggests that various factors, each related to the specific nature of the performance, partially alleviate the effects of loss of set. For example, practice swings of a tennis racket, a golf club, or a baseball bat may help to reinstate the motor programming or other cognitive and motor processes that will be involved in performance. Research also suggests that mental imagery and relaxation techniques may be useful in reducing the influences of warm-up decrement.

Watch an NBA player take a free throw shot. Before each shot, the player may do one or more of the following: dribble the ball, take a deep breath, mentally imagine the flight of the ball going through the hoop, or take a practice shot without the ball. The player's preshot routine is highly practiced and repeated almost exactly the same way on each occasion. The exact effect of the preshot routine has been debated for years, but the evidence of it having a positive effect on performance is very strong (see "The Preshot Routine" in chapter 6). The reduction of warm-up decrement very likely accounts for some of this effect.

SELF-DIRECTED LEARNING ACTIVITIES

1. Define the terms *warm-up decrement* and *set* in your own words.
2. Describe three situations in the recent past in which you have personally experienced warm-up decrement.
3. What kinds of activities do you think you could have performed to help you avoid the periods of warm-up decrement you described in question 2?
4. Design a research methodology to specifically examine the occurrence of warm-up decrement in performance, and an experimental treatment that could be undertaken prior to performance to alleviate these detrimental effects.

NOTES

- Namikas (1983) noted that Thorndike's comment might have been one of the first documented observations of warm-up decrement in the literature.

Namikas, G. (1983). Vertical processes and motor performance. In R.A. Magill (Ed.), *Memory and control of action* (pp. 145-165). Amsterdam: Elsevier.

- At the time of the basketball study, there was no three-point line. Therefore, all fouls in the act of shooting were two-shot fouls.

SUGGESTED READINGS

Adams, J.A. (1961). The second facet of forgetting: A review of warm-up decrement. *Psychological Bulletin, 58,* 257-273.

Schmidt, R.A., & Lee, T.D. (2011). Retention and transfer. In *Motor control and learning: A behavioral emphasis* (5th ed., pp. 461-490). Champaign, IL: Human Kinetics.

Schmidt, R.A., & Wrisberg, C.A. (1971). The activity-set hypothesis for warm-up decrement in a movement-speed task. *Journal of Motor Behavior, 3,* 318-325.

How are motor skills
stored in memory?

Why is it that some actions are remembered well for long periods without being performed, whereas others are forgotten quickly? Riding a bicycle is the classic example of a skill that seems to be retained forever once it has been learned. I can get on a bicycle after many years of not riding one, and my ability to stay upright and get to where I want to go is seemingly unimpaired. And yet, the key presses that I used to make a phone call just a few moments ago are almost completely forgotten if I want to call the same person again. What is it about how we store and retain memories that makes it easy or difficult to remember motor skills?

Perhaps one of the first things to consider in answering this question is the not-so-obvious one: Which motor skills do we really *want* to remember? For skills such as riding a bicycle, fly casting, operating a lathe, performing surgery, and driving a car, it is obvious that we would want to have good retention. This would be a positive attribute of memory. On the other hand, remembering the exact sequence of keys that I just typed moments ago would appear to be a frivolous attribute of memory, and perhaps detrimental too. Clearly, it is important that I remember the skill of typing. But, potentially, a good memory could interfere with performance in the future if I retained a strong recollection of my immediate typing experiences.

The stories "The Keypad" (in chapter 10) and "H.M." (later in this chapter) address the memory attributes of two patients who had suffered different brain impairments. In "The Keypad" I discussed an amnesic patient who played some rounds of golf with neuropsychologist Dan Schacter. The patient had a good memory for the golf swing, and he continued to play as well after becoming amnesic as he had before. On the other hand, the patient had severe difficulty remembering some of the things that average golfers take for granted, such as where he had hit his golf shot and even whether or not he had hit his shot.

Remembering where you hit your golf shot is really only important for a short period of time. After you hit your next shot, the memory of the previous location of your ball is irrelevant. It is similar to remembering where you parked your car. I don't want to remember where I parked my car yesterday; I want to remember where I parked it this morning. In fact, it might be easier to remember where you parked your car this morning if you forgot where you parked it yesterday, because the older memory might interfere with the retrieval of the newer memory.

The same can be said for the retention and performance of some motor skills. A simple experiment performed by David Rosenbaum and colleagues some years ago provides a wonderful demonstration of the concept that retention can, at times, either enhance or degrade performance. Rosenbaum's subjects were asked to simply say out loud a short string of letters of the alphabet (e.g., ABCD), and then to keep repeating that string as fast as possible for a period of time (e.g., ABCDABCDABCD). The twist here was that the subjects were asked to alternate between shouting and whispering the letters. You can demonstrate the task easily: start by shouting A, then whispering B, shouting C, and whispering D. Then repeat the string by continuing to alternate shouting and whispering. Notice that for a string of even-numbered letters (4 = AbCd, 6 = AbCdEf, 8 = AbCdEfGh, where a capitalized letter is shouted and a lowercase letter is whispered), the same letters are always vocalized in the same way (i.e., the same letters are either shouted or whispered). Rosenbaum's subjects found this easy to do and could vocalize many letters in a short period of time. Rosenbaum then asked his subjects to produce odd-numbered strings (e.g., 3 = AbC, 5 = AbCdE, 7 = AbCdEfG). Try this yourself, alternately shouting and whispering each subsequent letter for a three-letter string (e.g., AbCaBcAbCaBc). You will find very quickly that this task is much more difficult because once you finish a string of letters and start over again, the letters that were previously shouted loudly now must be whispered, and vice versa.

The conclusion from the Rosenbaum experiment is that the memory for how you previously spoke the letter could either facilitate performance (i.e., for even-numbered letter strings) or hinder performance (i.e., for odd-numbered letter strings). But that is not the whole story. Try the task again, but now cycle through several repetitions of a very long even-numbered string (i.e., the entire alphabet: AbCd . . . WxYzAbCd . .), again alternating shouts and whispers, and compare your performance with that of repeating a very long odd-numbered string (i.e., the entire alphabet minus the letter Z: AbCd . . . WxYaBcD . .). What you will probably find is that speed of vocalizations is about the same, regardless of whether the string was odd or even. For long strings, the retention of how you previously spoke the letter A has vanished, and so too has the positive and negative effects on performance.

Because the memory for the short string had a strong influence on performance, a logical conclusion is that the memory facilitated performance when the remembered vocalization was used again as before, but degraded performance when it interfered with the required (opposite) vocal stress. However, because the memory for the long string had deteriorated by the time the end of the string was reached, there was no longer a facilitation effect, but neither was there an interference effect. It seems as though the specific motor command for shouting a letter is remembered only for a brief period of time, during which the memory can have either a positive or negative effect on subsequent performance.

So, what does all this say about why some skills are retained only for brief periods of time, whereas others are retained for quite long periods of time? For this question, let's consider another experiment, this one by neuroscientist Stephan Swinnen. Subjects in this research practiced a relatively simple task: rapidly flexing, extending, and flexing the elbow, the start and finish of this three-component movement was to be completed in exactly 650 milliseconds. After learning this task, his subjects performed retention tests after delays of several minutes up to five months. The results were intriguing. The subjects lost all capability to perform the task in the exact goal time (650 msec). However, the rhythm (or relative timing) with which they had learned to flex, extend, and then flex the elbow was retained very well. There appeared to be dissociated effects for the memory of the timing aspects of this task: the rhythm was retained well, but the specific goal time was not.

These and other research findings have led researchers to speculate that motor skills are not learned and stored as a single representation in memory. Different attributes of a motor skill may be stored as separate memory representations. Further, we can speculate that each of these representations has unique retention characteristics; some attributes are retained well for a very long time, and others are retained for only very brief periods of time. When the performance of a particular motor skill is required, it is likely that a person draws on multiple memories to regulate movement control. What one observes in a performance reflects the combined strengths of all the memories.

In the case of riding a bicycle, the characteristics of memory that permit us to stay upright and move forward are the most important and likely remembered very well. This is why it appears that we retain the skill of bike riding forever. However, other features, perhaps less noticeable and not important for staying upright and moving forward, may be retained much less well, such as the efficiency of effort or power. The loss of these memory features may reduce your efficiency but won't make you fall over.

SELF-DIRECTED LEARNING ACTIVITIES

1. Define the term *forgetting* in your own words.
2. Pick a sport task and describe the types of skills required for it that are typically either forgotten rapidly or retained very well.
3. Ask a friend to perform Rosenbaum's letter-vocalizing memory experiment, described in the story, using strings of 4, 5, 6, 7, 25, and 26 letters. What do your results suggest about the effect of memory on performance?
4. Create an adaptation of Rosenbaum's memory experiment using a task not mentioned in the story. For example, one task would be to have subjects alternate playing notes softly and loudly on a piano. Be creative.

SUGGESTED READINGS

Rosenbaum, D.A., Weber, R.J., Hazelett, W.M., & Hindorff, V. (1986). The parameter remapping effect in human performance: Evidence from tongue twisters and finger fumblers. *Journal of Memory and Language, 25,* 710-725.

Schmidt, R.A., & Lee, T.D. (2011). Retention and transfer. In *Motor control and learning: A behavioral emphasis* (5th ed., pp. 461-490). Champaign, IL: Human Kinetics.

Swinnen, S.P. (1988). *Learning and long-term retention of absolute and relative time.* Unpublished manuscript, Catholic University of Leuven, Belgium.

H.M.

What does the amnesia suffered by Henry Gustav Molaison reveal about memory and motor skills?

For over 50 years he was known in the literature as Henry M., or more commonly, simply as H.M. In 1953, at the age of 27, Henry Gustav Molaison underwent an operation to relieve the debilitating effects of epileptic seizures. The neurosurgeon, William Scoville, removed portions of H.M.'s medial temporal lobes. The surgery was a success in terms of reducing the frequency of the seizures. However, the operation left H.M. with severe amnesia; he could remember things from before 1953, but from that point on he could not form new memories. Over the next 55 years H.M. generated considerable fascination among scientists who were interested in understanding how and why the brain creates some memories but fails to create others. In the story "The Keypad" in chapter 10, I discussed the fact that some people with amnesia can perform previously learned motor skills without much apparent degradation in performance. H.M. represented a rather different case: he could learn new motor skills but had difficulty learning or remembering many other types of information.

Some of the initial experiments in which H.M. was a participant were conducted by Brenda Milner and Suzanne Corkin. These experiments showed some remarkable dissociations in his ability to learn and remember new information. For example, H.M. showed essentially no memory for items that had been shown to him only a few moments earlier (such as prose passages, pictures of faces, and word pairs). Of great surprise to the researchers, however, was the fact that H.M. showed session-to-session improvements in motor learning tasks, such as pursuit tracking and mirror tracing. Moreover, H.M. had good retention of the mirror-tracing task when tested again almost a year later. Perhaps the most astounding finding of all, however, was that H.M. showed retention of these motor skills even though he could not remember ever having practiced them. In fact, he did not remember the names or even the faces of the researchers with whom he had done these experiments.

One explanation for why H.M. could learn motor skills but not other types of information may relate to the differences between explicit and implicit processes, which were discussed in chapter 10 (see "The Keypad"). Explicit processes refer primarily to verbalizable information, which can be remembered in detail (and thus are sometimes called explicit memories). Implicit processes refer to the nonverbalizable procedures that support performance on many tasks, but which are not normally available for detailed recall. One suggestion is that the operation performed on H.M. left a permanently impaired ability to form explicit memories, but left implicit processes intact.

The explanation for the explicit/implicit process dissociation is a gross oversimplification of an incredibly complex network of neural processes that underlies our capability to function. An interesting personal aspect of H.M. was his willingness to serve as a participant in many experiments over the 50-plus years that he had his disability. Although he did not understand why, H.M. somehow realized that his participation in research was important. As Suzanne Corkin explained, "He is altruistic: when I asked him to tell me about Dr. Scoville (with whom H.M. had several appointments before his operation), he said, 'He did medical research on people—all kinds of people. What he learned about me helped others too, and I'm glad about that.'" H.M. promised that his body would be available for further neurological examination upon his death, which occurred in 2008. These examinations are ongoing and may help scientists uncover more of the mysteries of H.M.'s brain.

SELF-DIRECTED LEARNING ACTIVITIES

1. Explain amnesia in your own words.
2. What is a memory dissociation? Look up the term if you are not familiar with it and discuss why it is especially revealing about the working of the brain.
3. Compare and contrast the memory impairments of H.M. with the memory impairments of the amnesic patient discussed in "The Keypad."

NOTES

- H.M. died on December 2, 2008.
  www.nytimes.com/2008/12/05/us/05hm.html

SUGGESTED READINGS

Corkin, S. (2002) What's new with the amnesic patient H.M.? *Nature Reviews Neuroscience, 3,* 153-160.

Milner, B., Corkin, S., & Teuber, H.-L. (1968). Further analysis of the hippocampal syndrome: 14-year follow-up study of H.M. *Neuropsychologia, 6,* 215-234.

Schmidt, R.A., & Lee, T.D. (2011). Retention and transfer. In *Motor control and learning: A behavioral emphasis* (5th ed., pp. 461-490). Champaign, IL: Human Kinetics.

Author Index

Note: Though references to it are not included in this index, *Motor control and Learning: A Behavioral Emphasis* by Richard A. Schmidt and Timothy D. Lee provides helpful background information for most of the scenarios in this book.

A

Abernethy, B. 202, 204
Adams, J.A. 111, 216, 217
Alexander, R.M. 159
Anderson, M.C. 37
Ashbaugh, D. 151

B

Barber, P.J. 15
Becklen, R. 42
Beilock, S.L. 34, 35, 36, 37, 107, 108
Beltzner, M.A. 8
Bernstein, N.A. 156
Bjork, R.A. 186, 189
Blakemore, S.J. 140, 141
Bradley, J. 130
Brown, A.M. 90
Bruce, D. 60

C

Carson, R.G. 159
Castelli, J. 12
Castenada, B. 108
Cayleff, S.E. 173
Chabris, C.F. 41, 42
Chapanis, A. 73
Chase, W.G. 209, 210, 211
Chittka, L. 57
Christina, R.W. 93
Cochrane, A. 52, 54
Corkin, S. 223, 224
Crossman, E.R.F.W. 166, 167

Cuddy, L.J. 186

D

Dapena, J. 90
Darnell, M. 17, 21
Davids, K. 125
DeGroot, A.D. 209, 211
Dell, G.S. 60
Diedrich, F.J. 159
Drews, F.A. 116

E

Elliott, D. 131, 132, 133
Ericsson, K.A. 34, 37, 211

F

Fitts, P.M. 34, 37, 45, 46, 47, 48, 49, 53, 56, 57, 58, 127
Flanagan, J.R. 6, 8, 141
Flegal, K.E. 35, 37
Franks, I.M. 199

G

Gentner, D.R. 151
Gilovich, T. 76, 77
Gladwell, M. 36, 37
Gonso, S. 108
Gray, R. 37, 107, 108, 147
Groomer, L. 100, 102
Gzowski, P. 211

H

Hellström, J. 111

Helmuth, L.L. 113, 116
Henry, F.M. 79, 91, 92, 93, 145, 169, 170, 171, 172, 173
Henslin, J.M. 99, 101, 102
Heuer, H. 151
Hick, W.E. 56, 84
Hodges, N.J. 199
Horak, F.B. 154, 156
Horn, R.R. 199
Hoyt, D.F. 159
Hubbard, A.W. 96, 98
Hunt, P. 173

I

Ivry, R.B. 113, 116

J

Jacoby, L.L. 186
Janelle, C.M. 199
Johansson, G. 197, 199
Jordan, P. 15
Julin, A.L. 90

K

Kelso, J.A.S. 154, 156, 159
Khan, M.A. 133
Klein, R.M. 120

L

Langer, E.J. 100, 102
Lashley, K.S. 60, 61
Lee, T.D. 159, 186
Levin, D.T. 42
Lien, M.C. 120
Logan, G.D. 146, 147, 148

M

MacDonald, J. 7, 8
Magill, R.A. 186
Marchal Crespo, L. 193
McCann, P. 110, 111
McCartt, A.T. 116
McCullagh, P. 199
McGurk, H. 7, 8, 99
Miller, G.A. 61

Milner, B. 223, 224
Morgan, R.L. 184, 186

N

Namikas, G. 216, 217
Nashner, L.M. 154, 156
Neisser, U. 40, 42
Nilsson, P. 111

O

Oskarsson, A.T. 77

P

Park, R.J. 173
Perkins-Ceccato, N. 108
Pollard, J. 12
Posner, M.I. 58
Proctor, R.W. 15, 21, 22, 120
Profitt, D.R. 102

R

Reason, J. 26
Redelmeier, D.A. 116
Reinkensmeyer, D.J. 193
Rogers, D.E. 93
Rosenbaum, D.A. 61, 135, 136, 137, 220, 221, 222
Rosenblum, L.D. 8

S

Salmoni, A.W. 189
Savelsbergh, G.J.P. 95, 98
Schacter, D.L. 206, 207, 219
Schilling, M.F. 77
Schmidt, R.A. 9, 10, 12, 51, 52, 53, 54, 56, 57, 127, 152, 177, 188, 189, 217
Schwartz, L. 32
Seng, C.N. 96, 98
Shea, J.B. 184, 186
Sidaway, B. 193
Simon, D.A. 186
Simon, H.A. 209, 211
Simons, D.J. 40, 41, 42
Slater-Hammel, A.T. 145, 146, 148

Smethurst, C.J. 159
Southard, D. 100, 102
Stanton, N.A. 93
Starkes, J.L. 211
Stephen, L. 42
Sternberg, S. 92, 93
Stobbs, J. 52, 54
Sussman, E.D. 12
Swets, J.A. 32
Swinnen, S.P. 221, 222

T

Taylor, C.R. 159
Thomas, J.R. 70
Thorndike, E.L. 215
Tibshirani, R.J. 116
Tillman, M. 26
Turvey, M.T. 125

V

Valls-Solé, J. 88, 89, 90

Van Zandt, T. 15, 21
Von Helmholtz, H. 141
Vu, K.P.L. 22

W

Warren, W.H. 159
Weigelt, M. 137
Weiss, M.R. 199
Witt, J.K. 100, 101, 102
Wolpert, D.M. 141
Wood, J.M. 202, 204
Wrisberg, C.A. 217
Wulf, G. 108

Y

Young, M.S. 93

Z

Zacchino, N. 26

Subject Index

Note: Page numbers followed by an italicized *f* refer to the figure on that page.

A

all-around athlete
  definition 169
  general motor ability view 169
  Henry's view 171, 172
  statistical prediction 169, 170, 170*f*, 171, 171*f*
amnesia 206-207, 223-224
anticipation
  end-state comfort 135, 136
  hockey 203
  spatial 96, 97
  sprint start 87, 88, 88*f*, 89
  temporal 95, 96
antiphase. *See* bimanual coordination
athletics, track and field. *See* sprint start
attention
  action goals 113
  bimanual coordination 113, 114, 158
  capacity 114
  cell phone and driving 114
  divided attention 113
  driving expertise 115
  focus of 35-36, 105
  inattention 10, 39-42
  internal or external focus 106, 107
  limits 114
  selective 105-106
automaticity 34-35, 107, 157-158

B

balance 154-155, 171

baseball
  batting 96, 97, 143-146, 144*f*
  pitching 98, 188, 197
  umpire 31, 32
basketball. *See also* hot hand, psychological refractory period
  benefits of mental preparation 109
  choking 34
  fakes 117
  hot streaks 75
  prediction of success 76
  warm-up decrement 215
Beckham, David 197-199
behaviorism 59-60
Bell, Cool Papa 131-133
bicycling 206, 219-221
billiards 109
bimanual coordination
  antiphase vs. in-phase 155, 157, 159
  attention 113, 114, 158
  degrees of freedom 153, 153*f*, 154, 156
blocked practice 183-186
bowling
  performance vs. learning distinction 176
  stages of learning 106, 107
  streaks 77
braking
  errors 9-11
  motor program 91, 92
  reaction times 81-83, 91-93

C

calculator
  Fitts' Law 45, 49
  implicit memory 205, 205f, 206
ceiling fans 19-21
cell phones
  and driving 114, 115
  keypad layout 205, 205f
checked swing
  role of motor program 144f, 145, 146
  timing 143
chess 209-210
choking 33-37
chopsticks, using 165-167
Christie, Linford 87
Cleese, John 123-124
closed-loop control 127-129
computer menus 48-49
contextual interference 183-186
coordination
  bimanual 153, 153f, 154, 157, 159
  centipede fable 105
  degrees of freedom 153, 153f, 154, 156
curling 127-130
Crosby, Sidney 117

D

Darnell, Michael 18, 21
decision theory 25-26, 27-32
degrees of freedom
  coordinating 153, 153f, 154, 156
  redundancies 123, 124
desirable difficulty 185-186
dice rolling 75-77, 99-100
dictionary analogy 187-189
Disraeli, Benjamin 65
door handles 17-18
drag racing 89-90, 95-96
driving
  braking 81-84, 91-93
  perceptual illusion 5

sensory feedback 139
steering 153, 154
unintended acceleration 9-11
Drummond, Jon 88

E

end-state comfort effect 135-137
ergonomics 13-15, 17-22
errors. *See also* error scores, Schmidt's Law, unintended acceleration
  action 43-61
  attention 39-42
  decision 23-42
  identification 25
  looked-but-failed-to-see 39-42
  perceptual 3-22
  speech 59-61
  targeting 25
error scores
  absolute error 72-73
  constant error 71-73
  variable error 51-54, 71-73
expertise
  athletic 169, 172
  perceptual 198, 209, 210

F

fakes 117-120
feedback
  augmented 187-189
  inherent 187-189
  sensory 129-130, 139-141, 187
Fields, W.C. 201, 203
Fitts' Law
  application of 45, 48, 127
  defined 46, 47, 47f, 49
  speed—accuracy trade-off 56, 57
  vs. Schmidt's Law 53
football 209
force variability. *See* Schmidt's Law
friendly fire 25-26
Furyk, Jim 109

G

gait
  coordination 158, 159
  degrees of freedom 123, 124
  end-state comfort 135
gambler's fallacy 76-77
general motor ability 169-173
Gibson, Josh 131-133
golf
  choking 33, 33f, 35, 36
  errors 71, 72
  focus of attention 105, 107
  illusion of control 99
  implicit vs. explicit memory 206,
    207, 219
  motor program 143
  perception 100
  performance vs. learning distinc-
    tion 175-177
  practice 183, 185, 186
  preshot routine 109, 110, 110f,
    111
  Schmidt's Law 51-54
  training aids 191-193
Goosen, Retief 33
gorilla 39-42
Greene, Maurice 69-70
Gretzky, Wayne 203, 209-211
guidance
  augmented feedback 188, 189
  training aids 191-193

H

Hick's Law 56, 84
H.M. 223-224
hockey 117, 120, 209-211
horseshoes 77
hot hand 75-77, 100-101
  definition 75
  theories 75
human factors 13-15, 17-22

I

illusion of control 99-102

illusion, perceptual 99-102
  McGurk 7-8, 99
  Müller-Lyer 5, 5f
  Ponzo 7
  size-weight 5-8
  Titchener 7
inattention blindness 10, 39-42
information processing
  Hick's Law 56, 82-85
  model 92
  speed—accuracy trade-off 55, 85
information theory 56-57, 83-84
in-phase. See bimanual coordination
invariance 151

J

James, LeBron 185
Joyce, Jim 31-32

K

keypads 45-49, 205-207
keystroke dynamics 149-152
kinesthetic aftereffect 100

L

looked-but-failed-to-see accidents
    39-42

M

magic tricks 40-42
McEnroe, John 27-32
mean. See central tendency under
    statistics
median. See central tendency under
    statistics
memory
  implicit vs. explicit 205-207, 223-
    224
  long-term 219-221
  loss 215-217, 219-221
  prospective 136
  sensory 131-133
  short-term 136
Mickelson, Phil 33

modeling 197-199
Monty Python's Flying Circus 123-125
motor learning
  observational 197-199
  performance distinction, contrasted with 175-177, 184, 188, 192
  stages of 106-107, 165-167
motor program
  checked swing 145
  complexity 91-93
  generalized 149-152
  speech 59-60
  startled 89
  typing 147, 149, 150, 150*f*, 151
movement time 45-49, 171

N

Nash, Steve 117-119
Norman, Greg 33

O

open-loop control 128-129, 143-148

P

pedal misapplication error. *See* unintended acceleration
performance vs. learning distinction 175-177, 184, 188, 192
point-light display 197-199
point of no return 143-147
politics 67, 70
population stereotype 13-15
postural control 135-136
practice
  blocked vs. random 183-186
  curve 165-167
  deliberate 34
  effectiveness 179-180
  law of 165-167
preshot routine 109-111
Privalova, Irina 70
probability 75-77, 99-101
product design 13-15, 17-22

psychological refractory period
  definition 117
  reaction time 118, 118*f*, 119, 119*f*
  relationship to fakes in sport 117

R

random practice 183-186
reaction time 171
  Hick's Law 56, 83, 84
  sprint start 68, 69, 69*f*, 70, 81, 81*f*, 82, 88, 88*f*
  startle effects 88-89
  task complexity 91-93
  vs. anticipation 87-90
redundancies 123-125
relative timing 151
rugby 101
Ruth, Babe 169

S

Schmidt's Law
  curling 127
  golf putting 51, 52, 53, 53*f*, 54
  speed—accuracy trade-off 56, 57
Scoville, William 223-224
self-organization 157
signal detection theory. *See* decision theory
skilled perception 209-211
soccer 95-98, 197-199
Sorenstam, Annika 111
speech 59-61, 92
speed—accuracy trade-off
  Fitts' Law 45, 47, 49, 53, 56, 57
  Hick's Law 56
  Schmidt's Law 53, 54, 56, 57
Spoonerisms 59-61
sprint start
  anticipation 87, 88, 88*f*, 89, 90
  reaction time 68, 69, 69*f*, 70, 81, 82
standard deviation. *See* central tendency *under* statistics, variable error *under* error scores

statistics. *See also* error scores,
    gambler's fallacy
  central tendency 67-70
  correlation 170-172
  independence 75-77
  statistical significance 67-70
  streaks 75-77
  variability 51-54, 67-70, 158
stimulus–response compatibility
    13-15, 17-22
stove top layout 18-21
streaks in sport 75-77, 100-101

T

tennis
  decision theory 27-31, 28*f*, 29*f*,
    30*f*
  focus of attention 105-106
  observational learning 197
tickling 139-141
Tillman, Patrick 25-26
track and field athletics. *See* sprint
    start
training
  aids 191-193, 201-204
  methods 179-180, 183-186
  vision 201-203

typing 60, 147, 149-152

U

uncertainty. *See* information theory
unintended acceleration 1-2, 9-12,
    25

V

Van de Velde, Jean 33-37
variability 51-54, 71-73
Vaughan, Stevie Ray 34-36
vision and motor control 131-133,
    201-203

W

warm-up decrement 10, 110-111,
    215-217
Weir, Mike 109
Weller, George Russell 9-11
Wie, Michelle 175-177
Williams, Steve 143
wood cutting 71-73
Woods, Tiger 143

Z

Zaharias, Babe 169-173, 177
zero-sum games 179-180

About the Author

Timothy D. Lee, PhD, is a professor in the department of kinesiology at McMaster University in Hamilton, Ontario. Lee, whose research on practice and motor learning has been frequently cited, is the author of more than 80 research papers in peer-reviewed publications in the area of motor control and learning. He is also the coauthor, along with Richard Schmidt, of the seminal text *Motor Control and Learning: A Behavioral Emphasis,* now in its fifth edition.

Lee is the former president of the Canadian Society for Psychomotor Learning and Sport Psychology and also a former editor of both *Research Quarterly for Exercise and Sport* and *Journal of Motor Behavior.* As an amateur golfer, Lee was ranked 22nd among senior golfers in Ontario in 2010. He also enjoys playing right wing for the Dundas Oldtimer ice hockey team and is a blues music enthusiast. Tim and his wife, Laurie Wishart, reside in Ancaster, Ontario.

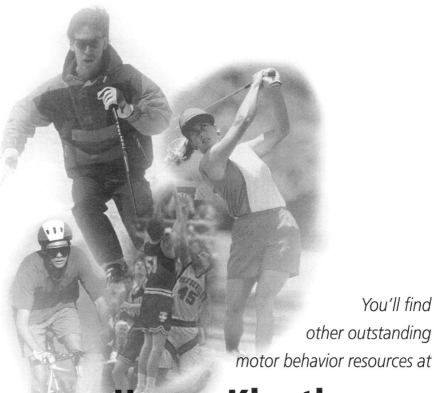

*You'll find
other outstanding
motor behavior resources at*

www.HumanKinetics.com

In the U.S. call

1-800-747-4457

Australia.............................. 08 8372 0999
Canada 1-800-465-7301
Europe......................+44 (0) 113 255 5665
New Zealand........................ 0800 222 062

HUMAN KINETICS
The Information Leader in Physical Activity & Health
P.O. Box 5076 • Champaign, IL 61825-5076 USA

LIBRARY, UNIVERSITY OF CHESTER